THE PASSION OF THE LAMB
GOD'S LOVE POURED OUT IN JESUS

Father Thomas Acklin, O.S.B.

SERVANT
BOOKS

PUBLISHED BY ST. ANTHONY MESSENGER PRESS
CINCINNATI, OHIO

Unless otherwise noted, Scripture passages have been taken from the *Revised Standard Version*, Catholic edition. Copyright 1946, 1952, 1971 by the Division of Christian Education of the National Council of Churches of Christ in the USA. Used by permission. All rights reserved.

Cover design by Brian Fowler
Cover photo by JupiterImages
Book design by Phillips Robinette, O.F.M.

LIBRARY OF CONGRESS CATALOGING-IN-PUBLICATION DATA

Acklin, Thomas, 1950-
  The passion of the Lamb : God's love poured out in Jesus / Thomas Acklin.
    p. cm.
  ISBN 0-86716-743-2 (pbk. : alk. paper) 1. Jesus Christ—Person and offices. 2. Catholic Church—Doctrines. I. Title.

BT203.A45 2006
232—dc22

                2005029282

ISBN-13 978-0-86716-743-6
ISBN-10 0-86716-743-2

Published by Servant Books, an imprint of St. Anthony Messenger Press.
28 W. Liberty St.
Cincinnati, OH 45202
www.AmericanCatholic.org

Printed in the United States of America.

Printed on acid-free paper.

06 07 08 09 10 5 4 3 2 1

Dedicated to all the little ones, the least and the last

Contents

ACKNOWLEDGMENTS

I would like to remember my Benedictine community of São Bento in Brazil, where I wrote this book, and the little brothers and sisters of the poor of Toca de Assis in Brazil. From both these communities I learned much about being little like a child.

I am also profoundly grateful to all my fellow monks at St. Vincent Archabbey in Latrobe, Pennsylvania, especially Archabbot Douglas Nowicki, Father Justin Matro and Father Boniface Hicks, who supported and encouraged me in many ways.

Sister Mary Ann, Patrick Doering, Scott Hahn, Mike Aquilina, Cindy Cavnar and Lucy Scholand all provided much inspiration and assistance.

Finally, to all the seminarians, students, directees, patients and friends who have shared themselves with me with such love, I in turn express my love and my gratitude for all you have taught me.

FOREWORD

Reading this book is a matter of life and death, and Father Thomas Acklin knows that. God led him to the writing, and God led you to the reading. Not a sparrow falls without His knowledge, and neither will a page turn without His guiding your hand and your heart.

The book begins by demonstrating the phenomenon Frank Sheed once described as "Christ in eclipse"—the sad fact that, at this turn in history, many of our contemporaries have forgotten Jesus or have never known Him. This real absence has replaced the Real Presence that lived at the heart of Christendom, and it has left a God-sized void at the heart of our culture.

Father Acklin shows us that void, in our institutions and in our hearts, and he does not spare us the pain that this knowledge will cause us. As a psychotherapist, he knows that such pain can mark the beginning of our healing. He also leads us to discover— or recover—the intimate presence of Jesus where it is most available to us, most healing and most efficacious: in the sacraments that Jesus established for this very purpose.

Again, as a psychotherapist, Father Acklin knows the importance of birth, childhood and nurture. He sees that Catholics receive these abundantly from Mother Church, but we often receive them ungratefully, or at least unmindfully—automatically. When we do, we run the grave risk of ritual presumption. Yes, the sacraments work *ex opere operato*—with or without our worthiness or cooperation—but their very gratuitousness implies a greater gravity. Of those to whom much has been given, Jesus said, much will be required (Luke 12:48).

And why should we respond grudgingly to Jesus Christ or to His Church? Indeed, why do we respond grudgingly? We all want to see Jesus (John 12:21). We all want to go to heaven. We just don't want to die in order to get there.

Yet so lavish is God's love for us that He has enabled us to see Him, gentle as a Lamb, and has welcomed us to go to heaven—even before we die. As Father Thomas shows us, we go to heaven whenever we go to Mass. We see Jesus! After reading this book, we'll never experience the Mass in the "same old way" again.

In my life I have read thousands of books, but few that burn with the passion of this one. Most of those were written by men and women canonized centuries ago. They are books that take you by the lapels and shake you. They seem to say: "Don't you see it? Can't you see what I see?" They are books whose every sentence could end with an exclamation point. And then, by the grace of God and the urgency of the prose, you do see what the author sees—or, rather, you see Whom the author sees. Then you know why the author is shaking you.

These pages shimmer with clarity and burn with passion. They are the words of a monk and a psychotherapist, but preeminently of a disciple who, through great love, has become a master—a spiritual master—a spiritual director—a director of souls. How blessed we are to have Father Thomas Acklin for a guide. For he leads where every heart yearns to go.

—Scott Hahn

CHAPTER ONE

IN SEARCH OF PASSION

Who do men say that the Son of Man is?… Who do you say that I am?" (Matthew 16:13, 15).

The urgency of this question comes not only from the nagging sense that we are on the brink of moral collapse but also from the voice of Jesus himself. Just when it seems that all traces of the Good News are forgotten and Jesus is but a historical memory, he stands on the horizon. His voice has a force that could not be coming simply from our wishful longings. It clearly is *his* voice.

In a homily on May 11, 1991, Pope John Paul II prophesied, "A new missionary age will arise, a new springtime for the Church."[1] We see signs of this new springtime already. Those drafting the constitution of the European Union did not want to mention the Christian roots of European civilization, but approval of that constitution evaporated. Meanwhile, the death of Pope John Paul II, one of the loudest voices calling for the recognition of the deepest meaning of human life, and the election of his successor, Pope Benedict XVI, drew millions of people to Rome and countless other millions to the television. One producer told me candidly that the networks did not want to cover so extensively the events at the Vatican but had to because of popular demand.

How can we understand the passionate love and devotion of those who traveled so far, waited so long, lived in the streets? And

what sense can we make of the fact that most of them were
the young?

At the same time, there is that nagging sense that we veer on
the brink of collapse, that malignant rot is in the marrow of the
bone, that all could explode in our faces. Daily news programs
report crisis after crisis: terrorist insurgencies, corruption and the
proliferation of weapons of mass destruction even in poor countries. Atheism seems to be spreading throughout the first-world
countries, accompanied by avowed Christians' diminished participation in their churches.

Even in more wholesomely Christian nations such as the
United States, politicians and ecclesiastical leaders invoke the sep-
aration of church and state and often consign moral issues to personal belief rather than public discussion. The legalization of
abortion, meant to keep the procedure "safe and rare," has led to
almost fifty million deaths of preborn children in the United
States alone.

The same nation watched Terry Schiavo die by having her
feeding tube removed, though there was no written account of her
own wishes, and those closest to her disagreed on what her wishes
were. Individual "choice" and "rights" have become the common
understanding of what constitutes morality, and Christians and
Catholics do not seem any more inclined than anyone else to
appeal to the teachings of the gospel or of the church for guidance
with respect to how they vote but also how they manage their
personal lives.

Back to the Question

What is perhaps most disturbing is the fact that discussions of
morality and religion seem to have little if anything to do with the
person of Jesus Christ. Somehow they seem abstract and philosophical or inviolably personal. If one asserts that there are truths

that hold for all people of all times, such passion is often dismissed as being too emotional or even fanatical.

To have passion about religious faith or about Jesus is likewise viewed suspiciously, even by the leadership of churches that call themselves Christian. Often this leadership has been as silent or as "pro-choice" as nonbelievers, and this has had the effect of making not only society but also certain Christian denominations appear to be post-Christian. It leaves one asking the question, are we living in a post-Christian age?

The Catholic church has taken a high-profile stand on many contemporary issues, such as the teaching of the pope and bishops regarding the dangers of the culture of death. The church has paid dearly for the force and clarity of this teaching, through undisguised anti-Catholicism and blatant discrimination, as well as in other forms of attack.

Strangely, many who have been raised Catholic have chosen not to leave the church in any clear way but to remain "within" while denying essential teachings of the church and demanding changes in structure and discipline. Sometimes leadership of the local churches has expressed less than a clear and strong unity with the teaching of the universal church. Weak or silent leadership sometimes is suspicious of any passionate desire for genuine renewal, while tolerating dissent and ambiguity.

Before we can decide if societies founded on Christian principles or if Christianity itself has become post-Christian, we must return to the question Jesus asked, "Who do you say that I am?" The echo of the question becomes even louder just when fantasies try to remake Jesus into a New Age prophet, to cut him down to our own size or philosophy. Meanwhile, news magazines promote "critical" studies that question whether there is any solid historical knowledge about who Jesus is or what he did.

It is impossible to be passionate about Jesus if we are unsure he ever existed or if we wonder whether his teachings make that much difference anyway. Indeed, what he taught has its force only in terms of who he is. The Gospels clearly point out that understanding who Jesus is requires a choice, a passionate choice that will change us completely.

Ultimately the passion of our Lord and Savior Jesus Christ is the fullest manifestation of what this choice is and what it means. For if we believe that his passion, death and Resurrection really took place, then *we* have to become passionate and take up our cross and follow him. Perhaps this is why we see such resistance to the belief that all of this really took place.

The really good news is that the more Jesus is handed over to the dispassionate myth of New Age religions or scourged by "new historical evidence" or "lack of evidence," the more insistently the question "Who do you say that I am?" echoes, and the more passion it generates. The more we cut Jesus down to our size, the more absurd this caricature of him becomes, and the more passionately he towers before us and stirs the passion within us. As Pope Benedict XVI insisted in his homily at his inauguration as the successor of Saint Peter, "the Church is alive!"[2]

About Passion

Depending on how you see it, passion usually has either a good name or a bad name. We want to live passionately, yet passion can overrun with emotion, causing us to act irresponsibly or even violently. Religious belief can rise passionate when confronted with an open attack upon it or an attempt to purify it.

As an analogy, I think of some of the statues that I have seen in my travels throughout Europe. Some of the images of Christ, the Blessed Mother, angels and saints, carved on some of the great cathedrals with loving, devoted artistic intricacy, were rendered headless centuries ago in some iconoclastic passion of reformation or rebellion. I have wondered at the enormous passion involved in their creation and in their destruction. We human beings are passionate, and passion will come out in one way or another, to build up or to tear down.

Christians and others have often tried to restrain or even mortify the passions in order to strengthen the will. Others have sought to set their passions free in order to find true freedom and fulfillment. Still others have found their passions burdensome. Consider Victor Hugo's hunchbacked bell ringer, who following his beloved's rejection looks in anguish at a gargoyle of Notre Dame and laments, "Oh! why am I not of stone, like thee?"[3]

Passion often involves suffering, which usually comes from the deepest and most personal kind of feeling. The Greek word *pathe* names this profound feeling. In English it is found in words like *sympathetic* (feeling with), *antipathetic* (feeling against someone or something) and *empathetic* (feeling almost as if one is inside someone else). The Latin verb for passion is *patior, pati, passus sum,* meaning "to suffer, to undergo, to submit to, to be patient, to lie open or be vulnerable."

It is true that passion can overrun us, that we "suffer" our passions and feelings. Yet Christian tradition has always insisted that we need passion in order to pursue what is good and true. Indeed, there can be no virtue without passion, since passion is the energy that is transformed into virtue.

As Saint Thomas Aquinas summarizes the Catholic faith on this point, unless the passions are formed and directed by the intellect, they are blind and even dangerous and sinful.[4] For our purposes here we will call blind passion *impulse.* But passion drives desire, and if passion is not blind but truly human, it must ultimately be directed toward the highest good, God. Every act of *human* free will must be aimed toward God.

Does it sound as if I just took all the fun out of passion and all the flame out of desire? Not really. It is very confusing and even frustrating for us, but the truth is that we humans need to have a certain distance, a certain space, between ourselves and the fulfillment of our desire. That's just the way we are made. Our human passion and desire will be endlessly and desperately frustrated and distorted if we seek satisfaction in things that are limited or finite.

Just look at the people who have plenty, whose every dream seems to be satisfied, yet who suffer from despair and long for fulfillment. Some people work their way through an ever-increasing wealth and an endless series of romances, becoming more and more restless. What is it we desire? Always "something else"!

We cannot find infinite meaning in what is finite. As Saint Augustine wrote in his *Confessions*, "The thought of you stirs him [the human person] so deeply that he cannot be content unless he praises you, because you made us for yourself and our hearts find no peace until they rest in you."[5]

Human desire needs to transcend itself, to stretch out passionately into the infinite, if there is ever to be some satisfaction in any person or thing, though even that satisfaction is limited. Indeed, the limits and boundaries of everyone and everything we know and enjoy, including our own selves, become the contours of what is most precious and unique about each individual. They define what is most intimately beautiful about each one of us, *if* and *only if* we desire and love them not as ends in themselves but in the unlimited beauty of our infinite God.

Flesh Wounds

Jesus did not come to make human desire irrelevant or to abolish desire; he came to fulfill it. Yet in fulfilling it he shows us much about ourselves, about human desire and about human love. To come to understand this is to come to know Jesus as the Christ, for it is impossible to know who Jesus is without passion: the passion of faith and the passion Christ lived out in his life and ministry, which culminated in his passion and death on the cross.

The tendency to cut Jesus down to our own size always involves a diminishment of the passion of Jesus Christ and a subsequent diversion from really getting to know him. It is truly amazing how strong our resistance to facing him and knowing him can be. From the moment Mel Gibson announced plans for the movie *The Passion of the Christ*, it was ever more apparent how ambivalent we can be when we have to "look on him whom [we] have pierced" (John 19:37b). There seemed to be endless reasons why one should not enter into this encounter with Christ's passion, including concerns about anti-Semitism, fundamentalism, naïve historicism and emotional devotion.

The reactions to this film, both positive and negative, show by their intensity how unsatisfied our human passion is. Only his passion can quench our thirst.

It is interesting to recall that the Latin verb *patior*, besides meaning "to suffer or feel deeply," also means "to lie open or be vulnerable." The word *vulnerability* comes from the Latin noun *vulnus, vulneris,* meaning "wound." To be vulnerable is to lie open, to be exposed to being wounded, and the wounds of Christ crucified are the emblems of his passion.

Not only our passion but also our vulnerability is a very important and personally intimate place of contact between Christ's life and our human lives, as well as between Christ's death and our own approach to death. In this sense we can extend the meaning of Christ's passion to include not only the last days and hours of his life, culminating in his death, but all the mysteries of his life, including his Resurrection. We see the vulnerability of the divine Son—of the infinite, divine Person—in his taking on a finite human form or nature, becoming one of us.

In the vulnerability of our own passion, we marvel at and share in the infinite vulnerability of his passion. We embrace our passion in embracing his, pressing our wounds against his.

Perhaps the greatest loneliness we can feel is that of needing to hide our vulnerability, to deny our wounds, to act as if we do not care, as if everything is fine. In my experiences as a psychotherapist and a spiritual director, I have had the privilege over and over again of seeing the relief of a person who finally is able to release feelings that he or she has always felt should not be there. I see this relief not only upon the face but spreading through the entire body. It often starts with a look of embarrassment, where earlier the person has not been able even to look at me. Often there is much pain and many tears. At other times he or she might begin to chuckle, then giggle, then be overwhelmed with laughter. The person usually apologizes shyly but, when invited to go ahead, shakes with laughter, gaining more rest from this than from a two-week paid vacation.

Often words are not necessary, at least at first. But then the need always unfolds to enflesh in our words and in our lives, in our actions and in our resolutions, the vulnerability that is the only way in which our deepest passions can emerge to be understood and realized. Then it is possible to allow our wounds to touch his wounds, to know the intimacy of his passion absorbing our woundedness and passion.

This means realizing that the desire to share in his passion is already the union with him we are seeking. Somehow the blood of my wounds and of my desire is already flowing into his wounds, and the blood of his wounds into mine.

One With Jesus

We must experience this as concretely as possible, not merely as an idea or as a vague intention. We have heard that we are to take up our cross and follow Christ, to join our sufferings to his. We will speak much about this in coming chapters. I would like to share here what I realized once in prayer, when I was particularly aware of my weakness and sinfulness and could see the sufferings my lack of love had brought to me and to others.

I was aware that I am forgiven but also that I persist in my self-centeredness and even in my sin. This caused me enormous grief and even fear of what sin I could commit in the future. Somehow, as if to try to guarantee that I would not sin this way again or suffer this way anymore, I wanted to bring my own sins to Christ crucified and join my sufferings with his.

As I have often done before, I imagined Christ hanging on his cross and myself somehow joining him on the cross, hanging there with him, even hanging there in his Person. This brought me some quiet and some peace. But suddenly the whole scenario changed.

I saw myself hanging alone on the cross, deservedly because of my sins and because of my refusal to love except selfishly. I was hanging there with reason, because of my sins, suffering because of my failure to love. Then *he* came and joined himself to me! He who knew no sin became sin and hung there with me, for me.

Suddenly I knew the "good thief" not as that lucky historical person mentioned in Saint Luke's Gospel but as *me*. I felt totally helpless, totally loved and totally vulnerable, and I knew that there was nothing to do but to accept this, to let him receive me. I saw that *his* wounds were my wounds!

We all seem to avoid being vulnerable. Is this because we do not want to see and know the truth about ourselves, our wounds, our sins? Are we afraid to experience the vulnerability of confessing our sins? Is this why the realistic depiction of Christ's passion is so hard to behold? Is this why the picture of an aborted human child or of a starving human being is so hard to look upon, because there we see the face of the suffering Christ and have to look at ourselves on his countenance?

Once, in the middle of a large and densely populated city in India, I was deeply distressed to gaze upon the protruding ribs of so many hungry people and to see the seemingly unemotional faces of so many crowded together, moving obliviously past each other. The scene seemed empty and absurd. As I stood there in the midst of these masses, my Christianity seemed useless, and my wish to do something to help totally incongruous and impotent. I cried out from somewhere deep inside myself, "Lord, what can I do?"

The calm answer came: "Just love me, there, here!"

If we are to love him here, we must become vulnerable in the vulnerability of his passion. If we wish to receive him and adore him in the abiding fruit of his love and his passion in the Eucharist, where the infinite Son of God lets himself be exposed and gives himself with unlimited vulnerability under the appearances of bread and wine, we must ourselves become vulnerable and live the passion of our vulnerability in the vulnerability of his passion. This is how all things will be made new, how every tear will be wiped away.

Indeed, we share in his suffering love and self-gift first by receiving him in the Eucharist, thus becoming one with him so that our lives become self-gift, so that we become self-gift in his self-gift. Then we see how we are to share in his passion in very personal ways in our lives.

To become vulnerable we must do as he has done—that is, become little and poor. How did he serve? How was he little and poor? Philippians 2:7 describes his *kenosis*: he "emptied himself, taking the form of a slave, being born in human likeness."

The only way we can share in his passion is by dying to self in his dying to himself. In a word, we must have faith, and in another word, we must become gifts ourselves as a participation in his self-gift. Only those who convert, who turn and become vulnerable like little children (see Matthew 10:15), can understand and share in the passion of this love, of this service. This is the passion of the new evangelization. ❧

CHAPTER TWO

THE PASSION OF THE NEW EVANGELIZATION

Go therefore and make disciples of all nations, baptizing them in the name of the Father and of the Son and of the Holy Spirit, teaching them to observe all that I have commanded you; and lo, I am with you always, to the close of the age" (Matthew 28:19–20).

At the onset of the new millennium, Pope John Paul II called for "a new evangelization."[1] It is a *new* evangelization because it makes all things new. This call summons up all the passion we have, a passion to truly touch the passion of our world, much of which has opted for a culture of death.

Is it any wonder that the young people have best understood this call of Pope John Paul? During his lengthy pontificate, Pope John Paul showed a Christlike love of youth, of children, not only because they are the future but because they are little and vulnerable. Our age has become too big for itself and takes itself far too seriously.

Here is the key to open the gate to a new evangelization through Christ's passion: We must learn to become little and simple; otherwise it is impossible for our passion to be in Jesus Christ and in his passion. We must take literally and realize explicitly and concretely the words of Jesus, "[W]hoever does not receive the kingdom of God like a child shall not enter it" (Luke 18:17).

Unless we are truly humble, passion will seem to us to be mere emotion. Unless we practice humility and live in humility, our faith will remain implicit rather than practical and vibrant. Unless we can see with the eyes of a little child, we will be blind.

Passion always wants to express itself, to act itself out, to become explicit. The *kenosis* of Christ resulted in his becoming incarnate. Passion does not hint around at what it wants but seeks to get what it desires, to concretize itself, to have a body, to become flesh. Yet as we will see, in being explicit, passion also requires patience.

The Meek Shall Inherit the Earth

The Catholic church has been a consistent voice insisting upon the truth of the gospel throughout the world in these confused times, particularly defending such issues as human life in all stages of its development. Now more than ever it is important that we not be afraid, that we respond to the grace that would preserve us from a failure of nerve so that the church continues to speak with the courage that Christ has given her and the Holy Spirit sustains in her.

A real persecution of the Catholic church in our times has created a hypersensitive caution over possible litigation and a dread of misrepresentation in the media. But we must not yield to the temptation to only hint at what we mean, in cautious statements made through a shield of spokespersons and screened by a phalanx of lawyers. The voices of the shepherds and surely those of the flock must become ever bolder and more insistent, ever clearer. And our voices must always be loving, so that, no matter how we are accused, we can never be guilty of hate mongering, no more than Christ can be.

We can find inspiration in looking back to the centuries in which Catholics enlisted in Crusades to regain the Holy Land and its sites from non-Christian conquerors. At the moment it is politically incorrect to suggest that there was Christian self-defense going on in the Crusades, whatever else went on. But in the midst of the various motives attributed to those efforts, stories have emerged of at least two small bands of lowly pilgrims who decided that they must save the Holy Land, the places where Jesus lived and died.

Legend has it that these bands were made up of children as young as six; thus the name "Children's Crusade." Some historians consider it more likely that the pilgrims were poor serfs and servants. In either case, we can say that they were "the little ones" of the world. Perhaps misguided or abused, they went forth in ignorance of what they faced. Many were slaughtered, others taken into slavery.

Was this all meaningless? In today's culture, victims can feel entitled to never forgive. Did these little ones even know they were victims?

My sense is that God may be calling the church in our times to be the new children's crusade. Jesus calls us to turn and become like little children. Is he calling us to be slain, as were these innocents, as were those King Herod killed in his paranoia, as were the fifty million aborted in the United States since 1973, victims of a lifestyle that had no room for them?

Will God call us to give our lives in witness to the passion, death and Resurrection of Our Lord Jesus Christ? It is not clear. God help us if we come to our demise in any way other than as little children. God help us if we die out because we keep our mouths shut or because we abort and contracept our posterity or simply die in our sleep.

Is it fair to suggest that many scandalous events in the church's history have occurred because her members have behaved in every way *but* like little children? The virgins caught without enough oil and the servants caught unready for the master's return have this in common: they were ill-disposed, caught posturing as something they were not.

No matter what we pretend to be, we are only children! The relief in admitting this is that we can be sure we have a heavenly Father. Though we know deep down that we are "illegitimate"—in the sense that we all are "captive to the law of sin" (Romans 7:23)—we know our loving Father has adopted us, has made us his own.

Be Not Afraid!

We are only little ones, yet so much is expected of us! Actually, no more than of the birds of the air or the flowers of the field.

Love sacrifices as Christ sacrificed. Sometimes death is required, and along the way it can mean sacrificing things such as tax-exempt status so that we can say what we really mean with genuine passion. Often the gospel proclamation involves even persecution, in little ways or greater ones.

Let's not pretend the persecution is not happening, and let's not be surprised that it is happening. Jesus warned his followers that we should expect attack and criticism from unfriendly and even hostile quarters. Jesus' warning should intensify our efforts toward passionate evangelization. To the extent that we experience persecution and sacrifice, we must be doing something right!

We need to remember and be strengthened by the oft-repeated message of Pope John Paul II throughout his long pontificate: "Be not afraid!" This message, which we also hear in Scripture—for example, from the angels announcing the birth of Christ and from Jesus when he appeared to his disciples the evening after he rose from the dead—must be the way in which Christians greet each other.

Our times have witnessed the sweeping growth of evangelical Christian movements throughout the world, often attracting people because the Christ they present is living and passionate. People hunger for passionate and life-changing decision. Strangely, such approaches to Christianity sometimes are at home with promises of comfort and prosperity instead of the cross which is somehow viewed as a thing of the past.

The loss of Catholics to such sects, particularly in traditionally Catholic countries, is well documented. Is it the appeal of sacrifice or of prosperity that pulls people to these groups?

Certainly the Catholic church must become an even more radical and powerful witness in a world turned materialistic and secular. We must not become "at home" with the culture, especially to the point of no longer being able to challenge it. Is our faith a cultural adornment like a winter coat that can be put on when the weather calls for it? Or are we willing to live and die for what we profess?

The Holy, the Beautiful and the Sacred

Our times have also witnessed a resurgence of religiosity of another sort, one that is not Christian, often described as "New Age." The tendency of New Age worship is to engage the deep human mystical need for participation and for an experience of God which contemporary worship often lacks.

There is actually nothing "new" about the New Age movement. Many eventually heretical sects developed within Christianity over the years, most notably the phenomenon of Gnosticism in the earliest centuries of the church. Gnostics believe in God but not in the personal God whom we know as Father. Much of New Age religion is simply Gnosticism revisited, but looking outside Christianity for its passion.

People looking to New Age cults are often looking for the passion that human hearts naturally long to pursue. The past decades have seen devotion suppressed in the church in a way that emphasizes what is beautiful but not what is sacred. Some liturgical reform has progressed in the direction of the mundane. Perhaps more than ever there is a passionate need for deep devotion and the liturgical experience of what is sacred, holy and beautiful. The search for the holy has led many faithful Christians to the Orthodox churches or to celebrations of the Tridentine Mass.

What are people seeking here? Accusations of nostalgia and of obsession with externals apply to some. But one of the seemingly innocuous reasons why Catholics abandon the practice of their faith is the lack of awe and reverence in the celebration of the liturgy. In a world bereft of roots or tradition, in a world of fast food and throwaway clothes, where is the sacred? Sure, McDonald's has fast food, and *USA Today* has fast news, but does the Roman Catholic church need to supply fast Mass? We want to see Jesus!

I really looked up to the priest in my home parish when I was a boy, and I still carry his memorial card in my breviary at the page for the *Magnificat.* Only years later did I realize what was special about him. He did not say Mass or read the Mass; he *prayed* the Mass. At the age of ten, I somehow knew this was different from other Masses I had attended.

Looking back, I think I projected onto this priest in all his ordinariness (he was actually very shy and a bit homely) everything I was looking for in a servant of God. It turns out he was not up to all of my projections. He was a lousy administrator, unable to bring together the people of a newly established parish to build and pay for a new church.

Yet when Father stepped into the pulpit, he preached. Even more importantly, when he ascended the steps to the altar, he prayed. In his life as well as in his celebration of the Eucharist, there was the sacred and the holy, and in his homeliness there was the beautiful. No one knew until he died, without enough money left to bury him, that he had given all he had to the indigent who came to the door of his rectory, a way of life undoubtedly prompted by his simple prayer.

We are starved for the beautiful, and we crave the sacred and the holy. They can never be domesticated, never kept in a fixed location or controlled. We find them in the Incarnation of the Eternal Word. The sacraments allow us to share concretely and explicitly in them still and to be transformed.

Real Transformation

The intellect is so made as to be able to order our passion, direct it toward God and ultimately shape it in selfless love. Yet what happens when the faith seems reducible to many words with no silence to assimilate them, when liturgical correctness suppresses beauty and living tradition and, worst of all, when scholarly theology and exegesis reduce the Christ of faith to bits of scattered data? Passion dies if it does not protest the dissection that turns faith in the living Lord Jesus into an autopsy of his corpse, washed up along the shores of time. Such an approach to Jesus, in teaching and in worship, gives people stones when they are hungry for the bread of life.

The new evangelization is necessary in these times, since there is a passionate need for the truth to be made explicit—not black and white but *explicit*. The Word became flesh, and the transformation coming through the Word must take flesh in us, must be seen as real.

We are witnessing in the church today—not merely as a human reaction to this need but more importantly through the power of the Holy Spirit—an incredible renewal of devotion to

Christ, often through his passion. Witness the devotion to the Divine Mercy as revealed to Saint Faustina and that to the wounds of Christ through Saint Padre Pio. In earlier centuries the still popular devotions to the Sacred Heart of Jesus and to the stigmata of Saint Francis had this effect of directing human souls to a deeper faith in and love for Christ.

Lay renewal movements and prayer groups often champion eucharistic and Marian spirituality, while clergy and educated Catholics sometimes eye such devotions suspiciously or even arrogantly. Sadly, these are the people who could provide the guidance and leadership these groups need. They could help integrate passion into the fullness of tradition and of liturgical life in a way that intensifies rather than suppresses devotion.

But the source of renewal movements and their naïveté should not surprise us. Again, it is so often through the little ones that the Spirit works, and the simplicity of their faith and devotion is a precious gift to the church, born as it is of passion. There is much more than nostalgia at work. In our times we hear a cry for a deep, explicit and concrete participation in the Word made flesh. ❧

CHAPTER THREE

BORN AGAIN

"Truly, truly, I say to you, unless one is born anew, he cannot see the kingdom of God" (John 3:3–6).

I remember the confusion about four decades ago when the charismatic movement swept through the Catholic church in the United States. How could a Catholic, baptized probably since infancy, be baptized again in the Spirit?

I heard various answers to this question, and though I was never deeply involved in the charismatic movement—being quieter and more contemplative by nature, at least when it comes to prayer—it always made perfect sense to me that we could be "baptized" again in ways that would unleash the original graces of the sacrament of baptism. Jesus himself pointed out to Nicodemus the need for a person to be "born again," not literally going back into his mother's womb but being born again in the Spirit (see John 3:3–6).

One of the reasons the charismatic movement caught on in the church with such great fervor and initial force was because it was so passionate. It summoned everything in a person and, through profound conversion, set everything on a whole new foundation in the Spirit.

It is astonishing how many members of generation X, Y, E— or whatever other designation is presently being applied to those thirty-five and under—have come to a zealous practice of the

Catholic faith not from being raised in the church but through a conversion later in life, often coming through the Blessed Sacrament and Marian devotion. What is evident in them too is their passion, the childlike way in which—often worldly wise and having pursued a fairly sinful life under the strong influence of sex, drugs or alcohol—they start anew, as if born again.

We see them armed with the *Catechism of the Catholic Church,* protected with scapulars and medals, loving Jesus and Mary, and looking for opportunities to go to Mass and confession and to adore the exposed Blessed Sacrament. If they enter religious life or the seminary, they usually are drawn to renewal orders or to dioceses whose bishops teach boldly in conformity to Catholic dogma. They have great love for the pope and interest in his teachings.

Childlike Faith

It is unfortunate when cradle Catholics or educated believers scorn the naïveté of such conversion and faith, a scorn I suspect is not unlike the impatient mood of the apostles when they wanted to spare Jesus the onslaught of mothers bringing their little children to him to be blessed. But we are called instead to have the patience born of the passion. Interestingly, Jesus says, in the Douay Rheims translation, "*Suffer* the little children, and forbid them not to come unto me" (Matthew 19:14).

There is always something inescapably and irresistibly vulnerable and childlike about faith in Jesus Christ in its most passionate expression. We see it in those who are involved in learning about the faith for the first time or in teaching it to others, in those who have discovered the treasure of the word of God in sacred Scripture, in those gathered for a pro-life witness, such as praying outside an abortion mill, in those organizing perpetual adoration, in those caring for the homeless and poor and in those who have just rediscovered the role of Mary, the Mother of Jesus, in their lives.

This passion is precious, and we must not abuse it with attitudes of elitist superiority. If we effectively undermine the foundations of such fervent devotion by dismissing it or trying to strip away what may seem to us to be mere externals, the vulnerability of such little ones may turn into the suspicious defensiveness and hypervigilance we find in a child whose trust has been abused. Jesus said, "[W]hoever causes one of these little ones who believe in me to sin, it would be better for him to have a great millstone fastened round his neck and to be drowned in the depth of the sea" (Matthew 18:6).

Actually, we in the church have a lot to learn from these passionate souls. Many of us are caught in the same position as Nicodemus: Seated among the elders and doctors, we are supposed to be "experts" on all this rather than the ones who have questions. We face the embarrassing fact that we do not know what it is to be born again, much less how to do it or help others do it. Most of us go elsewhere to indulge our passion rather than bringing it into prayer or into the living of our faith. So we too, like Nicodemus, can be dumbfounded and wonder how, after all we have been through, we can ever become like little children.

Yet it is absolutely astonishing to see how insistently Jesus proclaimed this requirement and how concretely he demonstrated it! The meek will inherit the earth, the poor in spirit will have the kingdom of heaven, those who hunger and thirst for justice will be satisfied, and those who mourn will find comfort (see Matthew 5:1–12; Luke 6:20–22). The one who knows he is a sinner is justified (Luke 18:14). It is not the powerful but the lowly who are exalted. Indeed, those who humble themselves will be exalted, whereas those who exalt themselves will be humbled (Luke 14:11). The last shall be first, and the first shall be last

(Matthew 19:30). The ones who lead must serve all the rest (John 13:12–20).

If you would like to allow yourself a rich prayer based on the Scriptures, look in the Gospels for all the references to children, where they are spoken about and where they appear. Find where Jesus mentions the least, the lowest, the last, the outcasts, the poor, and see how pervasively they and their condition show what the Good News really is. The Beatitudes are the agenda not first for social action but for kingdom action, from which alone social action flows. This is truth action, love action, hope action! The meek and not the elite shall inherit the earth.

The Wound and the Womb

Like everything else in Christianity, the only way to understand faith is to do it. In both the Old and New Testaments faith is more a verb than a noun: Faith has to be done. How does one become born again, become a little child? Is it accomplished by going back into the womb?

In a certain very real sense, this is actually what takes place. Though I cannot literally go back into the womb of my mother, through baptism I am really in the womb of the tomb with Christ, buried with him so as to rise with him.

Moreover, his mother is our mother, and her womb is for us the place where our adoption is made real as we become one flesh with him who took on our flesh. Saint Louis de Montfort quoted another great saint in this regard: "Saint Augustine surpasses himself—and me—when he says that all the chosen ones are hidden in the womb of the Blessed Virgin, during this life, to be made into the image of the Son of God. There the good mother keeps them, nourishes them, cherishes them, and makes them grow until she bears them into glory after death."[1]

How do we make these realities concrete in our lives? Can we die and be buried, "hid with Christ in God," as Saint Paul says (Colossians 3:3)? Can we thus dwell in the womb of the tomb and taste the Resurrection? Can we dwell in oneness with Christ and all the members of his body in the womb of Mary, the Mother of God? Can this be real, perhaps more real than what we see as the realities of daily life?

Though we cannot literally regress to the earlier years of our lives, can we become like little children? Can we explicitly realize by how we live and see ourselves or, better, forget ourselves, that we are the last and the least?

If we live in that womb, not simply seeing it as a place to get out of, but as a place that we will never leave, we come to know it as where life is begotten eternally in the Father's eternal begetting of the Son. But the only way to live in this is to become sons and daughters of the Father, and the only way to become sons and daughters of the Father is in Christ, in the womb, in the lowest place.

One time in prayer I faced the Scripture passage where Jesus advises his listeners not to vie for the highest places at the head table but to go and take the lowest place (Luke 14:7–11). I was pondering the usual meaning one gets from this: how I had to be careful not to be proud or to pay too much attention to my rank or position or others' perceptions of me. Then the Lord seemed to be inviting me to be more explicit about this, to actually do what he says here.

I knew he probably wasn't asking me to actually go and take the seat farthest to the rear of the chapel in which I was praying alone. But I knew as well that he was asking for more than some sort of mental act of understanding the meaning of the text or recognizing some application to my life. He wanted a response from my whole heart, with passion.

So in my heart I went to the lowest place I could find. How sweet and quiet it was, though rather lonely at first—waiting there, listening there. It seemed as if a long time passed, and then I remembered the further promise of Jesus that the one who invited me will come and say, "Friend, go up higher" (Luke 14:10). At that moment in my prayer, there he was, very close, beckoning me to come not so much higher as closer.

The Lowest and the Last

Since then I usually enter into prayer in this way. I often feel almost as if this is too easy a way to pray, as if I am cheating or somehow manipulating Jesus by turning his own words back to him. But I know he does not mind, and that this is exactly what he intends to show me by these words. Eventually I have come to a sense that being in the lowest place is a call, and I have wondered what I was supposed to do.

Then it occurred to me that I could ask the favor of being the last one to be seated at his banquet table in his kingdom at the end of time, being the one responsible to be sure first of all that every other person has been seated. I don't know how that unsavory idea came into my head because often I have hurried to find my place at a banquet or other event to be sure there was a place for me. But this idea of being last to be seated in the kingdom seemed very intimate and sweet, so I tried to enter further into it. I pondered the awkwardness I have felt at a banquet when I had trouble finding the tag with my name, wondering if I had been forgotten. I asked now to be forgotten, to be the last one seated.

When I imagined myself taking the last seat, I felt the meaning of the words "The last will be first" (Matthew 20:16). At the same time I realized that others would be able to recognize that I was the last one. After a brief moment of basking in this glory, a bit reluctantly I knew that I had to be willing to be the last to be seated *and* to want no one to notice.

Later the Lord seemed to ask me not to take a seat at all but to be sure that the feet of every single one at table had been washed. Lest people see me and figure out that I was imitating him at the Last Supper, I then prayed to wash feet under the table, without having anyone realize I was doing it.

I recalled how he advises us not to blow trumpets when we fast and pray but to go to a hidden place, where only our Father can see. Yet he goes further: "Do not let your left hand know what your right hand is doing" (Matthew 6:3). So I should not even watch myself doing all this but forget myself!

The Passion of Self-Gift

I share this prayer experience at the risk of blowing my cover and losing the anonymity I prayed for! But I share it not because it is about me or a special grace for me but because I think the Lord led me to a place where he is leading all of us in one way or another. It is the turning to become like a little child. Somehow all of us must be last!

Little children, like big children, often fight to be first. Becoming last seems impossible unless we realize the relationship the Lord has assumed with each one of us as if each one of us is the only one.

One time I was speaking to a very childlike seminarian, new to deep prayer, who was struggling with how God saw him and how God loved him. This young man came from a rather large family, and the question of where or when the food, attention or love might run out had seemed a realistic one for him. In his adult years he found himself once again wanting to know what most children wonder about at one time or another: whether God loved the seminarian more or less than he loved others.

Great was this young man's confusion when he sensed in prayer that Jesus was telling the seminarian that he actually loved him best of all! This seemed to be what God was saying to him beyond any doubt. Yet he felt presumptuous and wondered if the devil was deceiving him, since how could this be?

As I listened, I found myself remembering an episode from my own childhood. The second of six children, one day I asked my mother which of the six of us she loved best. She said, without a second's pause, "I love each one of you best."

I was not satisfied with this answer, of course, but now I know that she was telling me a profound truth. God gives mothers and fathers the ability, should they choose to accept it, to love each one of their children in a unique way and to love each one best. This way of loving is a finite reflection of God's infinite way of loving. And so, remembering all this, I answered the childlike seminarian's question: "God loves you as if you were the only person in the world, and he loves each one of us that way."

Now, he probably wasn't satisfied with that answer at first either because you really have to become like a little child to understand these things. And you have to *live* the truth in passionate, childlike faith before you really become a little child.

The Good Shepherd leaves the ninety-nine sheep to go search for the one that is lost as if it were the only sheep in the flock; but he does this really for each of the other ninety-nine as well (see Matthew 18:12–14), for each of us needs sooner or later to be found. To know that I have a Shepherd who is that good and that loving means that first I have to recognize that I am the one who is lost. In this sense I am in the lowest place. And he loves me so much that he comes to seek me, the least, as if I am the only one.

Only when we recognize that we are lost and in the lowest place, when we pray there and wait there in childlike or "sheep-like" faith, will we realize that he has come to us! I remember walking through the countryside to a parish where I was going to celebrate Mass and seeing a little sheep that had somehow gotten out onto a little island in the middle of a river and did not know how to get back. I identified with that lost sheep.

I have tried never to forget, whatever heights of hard-won autonomy and expertise I reach, who I *really* am. Despite my constant efforts to assure myself of who I am and where I am, I am lost without my Shepherd. I can pray Psalm 23, "The Lord is my shepherd…," with great passion, and I can hear the other ninety-nine bleating along. And so we are born again, over and over again.

More about sheep and lambs later. ❧

CHAPTER FOUR

CHILDLIKE LOVING AND LIVING

"Suffer the little children, and forbid them not to come to me" (Matthew 19:14, Douay Rheims).

We are all called to be the least, though God loves us all as if each is the greatest. We are called to be last, though God loves us all as if each is first. The late Fred Rogers, favorite neighbor to generations of children young and old, had the practice, even with adults, of giving a gift not only to the person whose birthday was being celebrated but also to every guest at the party. What a strange warmth I felt the first time I saw him do this. After bestowing a few gifts on my companion, who was his good friend, he handed another carefully chosen gift to me. What a concrete enfleshment of the way God loves!

In Brazil there is a renewal community of Franciscan inspiration called Toca de Assis, founded by a diocesan seminarian who is now a priest, Padre Roberto José Lettieri. In the first twelve years of its foundation, the community attracted more than fifteen hundred members. These brothers and sisters work with the poorest of the poor throughout Brazil, often living in the streets with them.

I was invited to a birthday celebration of Padre Roberto. The brothers and sisters, hundreds of them, gathered from all over Brazil at the church in Campinas that the bishop had given for their use. It was an amazing experience to celebrate the Eucharist (which lasted for hours) with these hundreds of little brothers and sisters of the poor, one more childlike than the next. They had brought with them the poor, many of whom were demented by drugs, alcohol or exposure and who could not keep quiet. These often cried out, seemingly with great happiness. I believe the kingdom of heaven is going to be very much like that celebration.

It should not come as a surprise that each of the houses of this renewal community has perpetual adoration of the Eucharist. Such childlike faith will renew the church and can renew us.

Fresh Starts

So it is no longer difficult for me to understand the need to be "baptized" again and again in the Spirit, renewing my sacramental baptism by being allowed to start all over again, to be born again. This is precisely why the Lord gave us the sacraments. Indeed, every celebration of the sacrament of reconciliation is a rebirth, a starting over. Each celebration of the Eucharist joins me anew with all the other members of the body of Christ, letting the Word who has become flesh enter me and deepen my oneness in him.

We never achieve the childlikeness to which God calls us, but we must enter into it over and over again, sometimes at great cost to our desire for control, our desire for achievement, our desire to firmly establish ourselves, to be great and independent. We approach this childlikeness only in union with Christ and his self-emptying love, his *kenosis.* Each time I go to pray, each new task I take up and each person I meet—again or for the first time—is an encounter with Jesus Christ, a new beginning.

Someone asked Mother Teresa how she managed to attend to so many afflicted, dying, poor people and still manage the affairs of her communities throughout the world. She answered with passion, "One Jesus at a time!"

Now, it is obvious to us that little children can seem very self-centered. They grab for security and love, unable to tolerate another child's having anything. A spoiled child can be particularly demanding, wanting everything now. This is childlike passion that is still impulsive. We are called to be little children, not big babies!

The childlikeness of which Jesus speaks is a *rebirth;* it requires dying so as to be born *again.* I must die and be reborn in Christ in order to be the child of which Jesus is speaking. Only by losing everything that I have can I be childlike in a self-giving rather than self-centered way.

Praying as Jesus Taught

The model for this giving is the widow who gave the most of all the donors to the temple because she gave everything she had, even what she had to live on (see Mark 12:41–44; Luke 21:1–4). She must have been born again as a little child, because giving everything requires all the passion one can muster.

It is necessary to actually go to the lowest place in one's heart to pray. Consider the tax collector who knew he was a sinner and could barely raise his eyes to say, "God, be merciful to me a sinner" (Luke 18:13). I must remember, however, that if I do not seek to *live* in this lowest place, I will probably not be able to *pray* there either, and vice versa.

It is the same with becoming self-gift. I should seek to offer everything I have to God, even what I have to live on and my very self. This is how Jesus taught us to pray, and how he himself prayed when he taught his disciples the Our Father and when he prayed alone in his final agony. Indeed, the only way to pray like this is to offer oneself in Jesus' self-offering.

It all comes down to seeking God's will rather than our own will, just as Jesus did in the garden of Gethsemane (see

Matthew 26:42; Mark 14:36; Luke 22:42). We trust *him* to give us our daily bread rather than trusting in ourselves. We ask for what we want and need, but we pray that this be realized only if it is his will.

To pray in this way, we need to take the eyes of our heart and mind and will away from ourselves and look to him alone. We can hold up in prayer the petitions and needs we have, for those we love and for ourselves, without letting them become our focus. Rather the *Lord* is our focus. As we pray in this way, humble and childlike, we are reborn again and again.

Such childlike trust, lived with passion, is the only way to live in peace. If I know who is the giver of everything I have and even of my life itself, what is there to cling to? How can I not offer everything to him, including my very self? These truths are meant to be lived passionately, not by accommodation, concretely and not theoretically, explicitly and not by some vague intention.

Most of our misery lies in our ever more desperate attempts to calculate and measure out love and trust, things that can never be calculated. These attempts kill passion. Jesus said, "No one has greater love than this, to lay down one's life for one's friends" (John 15:13, NRSV). This laying down is the lying open, with everything exposed and vulnerable, the vulnerability that is true passion. We understand this only as we participate in it.

Not doing this renders the gospel a mere ideology to be manipulated, studied perhaps and played with. Eventually, confronted with a little child or with true faith, we are unmasked as a new breed of Pharisee. Remember that in the time of Jesus the Pharisees were a renewal movement. They intended to observe the law even more fully and correctly, yet somehow they lost the passion of faith and degenerated into self-righteousness and even hypocrisy. Let's not let that happen to us. Let's lay hold of the passion of the gospel and live it to the full!

Suffer the Little Ones

What do those little ones look like, those who discover the way to enter the kingdom of our heavenly Father?

I do not know if the Lord's special grace is moving more powerfully these days to make people little and open to his goodness, or whether my own eyes are just able to see them more clearly. I meet more and more people in my life and certainly in my ministry who are simple, good, in some ways so pure and innocent. The strange thing is that many of them have, shall we say, been around the block. Actually, some have gone around the block again and again and even spent some time in the gutter.

How can we explain how persons who have been hurt and even abused can be so willing to forgive and so determined to follow God? Usually they still need healing and have a lot to learn. Often there are serious obstacles standing in the way of their deeper and more real love. Yet at the level of grace they stand ready, and they only need love, understanding and the opportunity to speak and to be heard in order for that grace to heal and free them.

How can I describe the awesome privilege of looking deeply into someone who is vulnerable, who is deliberately laying down the self-consciousness that burdens the rest of us? Eyes reveal more than words. Then there are the gestures, shy but not self-conscious, the readiness to cry and to laugh. Each one has his or her own little mannerisms that seem to reveal the very soul: a way of clearing the throat, of looking up earnestly to check and see how he or she is being heard, of turning the toes inward or rubbing one foot against the other, of scratching or pulling the hair in a particular way. Such gestures probably go far back into the earliest times of life.

This littleness has nothing to do with physical size or age. Indeed, the biggest ones can shrink most easily sometimes, and the aged and experienced can show depths of long-frustrated childlikeness. I have seen the hard and callous, those who want to come across as seasoned and wise, suddenly melt down to their basic elements. Their personas and other masks fall away, and they enter into a freedom that they had never been able to conquer by force. These are moments of sheer grace.

In all of this I come to recognize some characteristics of each little one that are absolutely unique and precious, and I learn to love them in these particular ways. In so doing I have no choice but to become more little myself. It seems to me that, in the intimacy of this kind of sharing, God allows me to participate in his way of loving. During those moments of vulnerability, I see how God loves each one of us as if each is the only person in the world.

Conversion as Shrinking

I am a psychoanalyst, and I have often been amused at being called a "shrink." Indeed, the kind of change to which we are called—our complete conversion to Christ—requires not only a shrinking of the mind but of the very self.

Jesus calls for this dying to self in the gospel. The one who would save his life will lose it, and the one who loses it will save it unto everlasting life (see Matthew 10:39). Saint John the Baptist described the decreasing taking place in him so that Jesus could increase (John 3:30). This is how we can be already dead and buried, as Saint Paul said, and still be living, loving and suffering with Christ and all the members of his body, indeed with all of creation (Romans 8:13; 14:7–8; 1 Corinthians 15:22; Galatians 2:20). We live on, now in Christ, by dying to ourselves, by letting ourselves shrink.

This can be very difficult for us to embrace. A lifetime of fresh starts, of resolutions that were never kept, conversions that grew old and changes that did not last can lead us to mistrust yet another life-changing conversion. Rather than giving up, we might ask ourselves whether we have been afraid and unwilling to be little.

How much have I relied primarily on myself when trying to follow through on the grace of conversion? Have I pressed on without really being intimately in relationship with the Lord, without whom there is no hope of faithful perseverance? Am I afraid to be little?

When I am out of sorts, perhaps anxious or a bit depressed, I check and see where my mind and heart have been. Have I been preoccupied with myself, with how I am feeling or being treated? Or have I had my eyes and my heart on the Lord and received everything, the good and the bad, in the light of his love? It is only in that light that I can understand what is happening and what I am to do about it.

It seems to me a fallacy to compare ourselves with animals in trying to understand our passion, to suggest that, in a way not so different from them, we are bound to a seemingly inevitable self-centeredness. So-called "lower" forms of life display an extraordinary attunement with what is beyond them in their life, but this is largely instinctual rather than free. Our enslavement is not our bondage to an animallike urge to self-preservation but a refusal to be truly human and to act freely and responsibly.

Whatever similarities we share with animals, we find our human fulfillment only in self-gift, and we fall from our human nature when we give in to impulses and fail to be passionate. Every misuse of our God-given freedom is based upon self-absorption. To rise beyond this is simply the human thing to do. Granted, original sin distorted our original creation, and we rise beyond self-absorption only with help from beyond ourselves, redemption through Christ.

Do Not Be Afraid!

We have the tendency to feel that something is wrong, seriously wrong, when we feel fragile, weak and in need of help. We naturally shrink from the feeling that the self is dying, yet what we need to do is to shrink into Christ in dying, becoming little, one of his sheep. The only way to live and to die without fear and dread is to live and die with Christ.

Death is, of course, the ultimate loss of self, and if we are afraid to die, we never truly live! Life has many "practice" deaths: We are always dying in the sense of aging and experiencing our limitations and incompleteness. Railing against these deaths is futile. If I try to "fulfill myself," I only realize that I am a bottomless pit. If, on the other hand, I passionately empty myself and give myself, then I find joy in the fullness of life.

My loss of self is tragic unless I freely give myself in Christ's self-gift. When I am not too self-conscious, not taking myself too seriously, then I can be like a little child and not like a self-centered big baby. I am free, and I laugh more and feel more deeply, though not about myself.

At our monastery in Brazil one year, shortly before Christmas, I was gazing at the crèche, the *praesaepio,* which had just been set up in our chapel. Two young monks were there with me, and they were as excited as two little children. One of them said, "There is no star over the manger yet." The other pointed to the empty manger, which would be occupied at midnight Mass the following night, and said, "Not yet. *He* is the star!"

If we become like little children on Christmas Eve, we can realize that around the altar are all the angels and saints. We can see their eternal life and prayers flowing into these moments of our time because his sacrifice of himself in love flows into these moments of time. The wood of the manger points to the wood of the cross; both are moments of infinite, self-giving love.

In giving all, being little, there is nothing to lose and nothing to fear. Pope Benedict XVI, in his homily at his inauguration as successor to Saint Peter on April 24, 2005, spoke especially to the young but to all of us:

> If we let Christ enter fully into our lives, if we open ourselves totally to him, are we not afraid that he might take something away from us? Are we not perhaps afraid to give up something significant, something unique, something that makes life so beautiful? Do we not then risk ending up diminished and deprived of our freedom?
>
> And once again the pope [John Paul II] said: No! If we let Christ into our lives, we lose nothing, nothing, absolutely nothing of what makes life free, beautiful and great. No! Only in this friendship are the doors of life opened wide. Only in this friendship is the great potential of human existence revealed. Only in this friendship do we experience beauty and liberation.
>
> And so, today, with great strength and great conviction, on the basis of a long personal experience of life, I say to you, dear young people: Do not be afraid of Christ! He takes nothing away, and he gives you everything. When we give ourselves to him, we receive a hundredfold in return. Yes, open wide the doors to Christ—and you will find true life. Amen.[1]

CHAPTER FIVE

FAITH THE SIZE OF A MUSTARD SEED

I thank thee, Father, Lord of heaven and earth, that thou hast hidden these things from the wise and understanding and revealed them to babes" (Matthew 11:25).

We tend to try to quantify and calculate, but Jesus turns all our calculations around. He tells us that the measure we use is the measure that will be used for us (see Matthew 7:2). And if we give our all, even though the amount might be small, it is more than enough (Mark 12:42–44).

When the apostles asked for more faith, Jesus told them it was not a question of more but once again a matter of being small. Faith the size of a mustard seed is enough (see Luke 17:5–6). Faith that small will grow into the greatest tree of all. It expands our hearts, like the yeast that causes the dough to rise (Luke 13:19–21).

In faith we invest our gifts and our talents (see Matthew 25:14–29), and this investment is what makes the difference, what makes the amount grow. The foolish virgins let their lamps burn out (Matthew 25:1–13), perhaps relying too much on their own fuel. We should have faith that there is oil enough. So are there wedding garments enough for everyone (Matthew 22:11–14), if only we put them on, being vigilant and poor, having no other business to occupy us than the moment of the Bridegroom's arrival.

This faith must be explicit. It has to go out to meet the Lord, crying out passionately with the humble, insistent plea of the blind man, "Son of David, have mercy on me!" (see Luke 18:35–43). Zacchaeus went to the effort of climbing a tree to see him (Luke 19:1–10), and the woman with the hemorrhage battled a jostling crowd in order to humbly touch the hem of his garment with faith (Luke 8:43–48).

All of these people and more went out, came forth, let themselves lie open in vulnerability. Jesus met them and recognized them explicitly for their faith in a way that brought conversion of heart and repentance and sometimes even physical healing.

Are we among those who try to silence such passionate outbursts for the sake of propriety? If we do not often see wonders in our own times and in our own lives and ministries, perhaps it is because we have lost the passion and the faith. Perhaps we are more concerned with being in control, being orderly and on time, than we are with meeting the Lord Jesus where he is and loving him passionately there.

Faith and Seeing

We read in Mark's Gospel about the rich young man who had kept the commandments all his life and came to Jesus in search of a greater perfection. The Gospel tells us that Jesus looked at him with love (see Mark 10:17–31).

The eyes have sometimes been called the windows of the soul. Surely they are the windows of transparency, of vulnerability. I am much less able to deceive someone who looks me in the eyes.

We often look away when the gaze of someone seems too penetrating, when we are not ready to read the unspoken words in the eyes of another. I turn my gaze sometimes in fear, when what I feel or what I see in the eyes of another is too great for me. In someone's eyes we can see and know and share his or her passion. We can be unmasked, laid open, exposed to the other person. The gaze can reveal so much.

Jesus surely searched, touched and healed with his gaze. And with it he strengthened faith the size of a mustard seed to confess all, to give all. Yet the Gospel tells us that the rich young man went away sad. He could not meet the gaze of Jesus. He could not give away his wealth in order to follow Jesus freely.

For us there are many kinds of wealth: always some sort of security, something we lay away. Jesus encourages us to travel light so that we will be able to see! This is the key to the meaning of the poverty, chastity and obedience to which he calls not only consecrated religious but all of us to some degree.

The insecurity we hold about ourselves is a kind of wealth in the sense that it can keep us from looking directly into the eyes of the Lord and of others. It can keep us from being free to follow the Lord wherever he leads. We can be stuck with lack of faith because we are too focused on ourselves. The resulting isolation keeps us from seeing ourselves in light of the Lord's love for us. So we cannot have faith in ourselves because we have lost faith in the Lord.

So much sin is based upon wanting to see something, someone, in such a way that we will be not only aroused but also reassured. But then, as some do when watching a movie with a particularly violent or frightening scene, we look away and close our eyes.

This is often evident to me when I see someone for spiritual direction or therapy. A rather brash young man used to lie on the couch and, following the psychoanalytic technique, I would sit behind him. Even though I could not see his face, he was only able to really open up when he knew I had turned away and was look-ing out the window.

A seminarian, now a very happy priest, would look up at me only furtively, otherwise looking down in shame. Shame and fear of intimacy kept him from making direct eye contact, and this in turn kept him from ever developing faith in himself, especially in his relationships with women, but most importantly in his rela-tionship with God. When we talked about what he called his "shy eyes," he would begin to look more directly at me and from there go more deeply into prayer and intimacy with God and others. He really had to practice this and, as he did, his faith in God and in himself grew, in that order.

Hidden Faith

But what about the words of Jesus at Saint Thomas' profession of faith, after allowing Thomas to see and to touch his wounds: "Have you believed because you have seen me? Blessed are those who have not seen and yet have come to believe" (John 20:29). The seeing happens with the eyes of the heart, with the eyes of faith in the unseen. We can also detect this faith in what is unseen by gazing into the eyes of another. C.S. Lewis commented that after he and his dying wife had exchanged their last good-byes and as she breathed her last, "She smiled, but not at me."[1]

Why does our relationship with God always emerge from and lead into the hidden, the unseen? Before the Fall, in the garden, the first man and woman seemed to enjoy a special intimacy with the Lord, who spoke with them and walked with them in the cool of the evening. This same Lord knew when they tried to hide them-selves from him (see Genesis 3). After original sin, what Pope John Paul has described in his theology of the body as the "original soli-tude" of each human being before God seems to have degenerated into a more oblique way of seeing and hearing him.[2]

From then on no one could see God and live (see Exodus 33:20; 19:20). When God called Moses from the burning bush, "Moses hid his face, for he was afraid to look at God" (Exodus 3:6). Moses could only look upon God from the rear (see Exodus 33:20–23). Later his direct communication with God would cause his countenance to become brilliant. He would veil his face when he was not speaking with God or conveying God's message to the people because they were afraid to gaze upon the brilliance of his countenance (see Exodus 34:29–35).

Finally God sent his Son, who is God in person yet is here also hidden, not simply in human appearance but in a human nature. The Son's Incarnation truly allowed him concrete human presence in history, and he assures us that whoever sees the Son sees the Father because the Son and the Father are one (see John 14:9–11).

Yet the Word incarnate died and rose in a glorified existence that we will someday share but do not yet understand. After appearing to various groups of people, he ascended to the right hand of his beloved Father and disappeared from sight (see Mark 16:19; Luke 24:51; Acts 1:9). He left us the Eucharist—his body and blood, soul and divinity, hidden under the appearances of bread and wine.

Then the Paraclete comes, but this seems to be a further advance into the unseen. We do not know from where he comes or where he goes (see John 3:8). We see him represented as a dove (Matthew 3:16; Luke 3:22; John 1:32) and revealing himself in tongues of fire and rushing wind (Acts 2:2–3). Though the Spirit dwells within all those who receive him, this dwelling within is hidden. Once again, God seems to be playing "hide and seek." This almost seems like a regression to the indirectness of the old law under which no one could see God nor represent him concretely.

A story is told of a child passing through that stage when there seems to be a ghost or something bad hiding everywhere, especially at night. One night, after the child had delayed bedtime as long as possible, after the mother had checked all the scary places in the closet and under the bed to show the child that there was nothing there, and after prayers had been said, the exasperated mother said, "Don't worry. Nothing can hurt you. God will stay with you and protect you." The anxious child responded, "But I want someone with me with skin on!"

With the Ascension of Jesus to the right hand of the Father and the descent of the Holy Spirit, are we once again left to search for a God "with skin on"?

In truth, the more hidden God becomes, the more he is deepening our intimacy with him. Throughout the history of salvation and throughout our individual lives, God is always leading us to look deeper, first with our physical eyes and then with the eyes of faith. Maybe the reason God is invisible is that he is absolutely transparent!

The faith that Jesus sought in those who followed him is this type of faith. Those who witnessed the signs and mighty works Jesus performed then were challenged to believe in the bread that comes down from heaven, to believe that they could eat his flesh and drink his blood and never be hungry again. They, like us, began to become very literal and thus to doubt. Many left him that day and did not follow him any more (see John 6).

One of the best witnesses to faith is Saint John the Baptist, the one who was sent to prepare the way for Jesus. Yet even John, after all those bold words calling for repentance, admitted that he was not sure who the Messiah really was. He sent some disciples to find out if Jesus indeed was the one who was to come (see Matthew 11:1–6; Luke 7:18–23).

Faith flickers as it burns, and ultimately the flame of faith is kept lit by the One who is the fire in Moses' burning bush. John was called, as he recognized, to decrease so that Jesus could increase (see John 3:30). So are we. This decreasing involves a dimming of the sight we have had until now so that we can see more clearly and in a more penetrating way with eyes of faith.

We must practice our faith and allow it to become more explicit so that we can truly see with its eyes. We must take up our cross and follow him, like a little child taking the hand of the trusted adult, and we must decrease so that he can increase. This is the freedom of the children of God.

Faith and Presence

Just when the Lord decreases to the point of vanishing, there is presence, the kind of presence we experience in transparency. This happened especially in his appearances after rising from the dead. Two disciples walked with Jesus to Emmaus, all the while thinking he was a stranger. Only when he vanished did they recognize his presence, how their hearts were burning within them as they listened to him (see Luke 24:13–35).

Mary Magdalene only recognized him in the garden when he called her by name. Even though she was not allowed to touch or cling to him, she knew his presence, and she knew that he was risen. Not even the doubts of those to whom she bore this good news could quench her joy and her faith.

It is certainly possible to live according to the criteria of empirical verifiability, as some philosophers have done, believing only what one can verify with the five senses. Yet why slice such a small piece from the cake? How will one ever understand transparency?

In the movie *A Beautiful Mind* a psychiatrist tries to explain to a woman the delusional system of her husband's paranoid schizophrenia: "It is horrible to lose those whom you love.

Imagine what he is going through, facing that they have never existed!"

Perhaps many of us have had the strange experience of being present and thinking we see, but not seeing. When I was a boy and my father would send me in search of some tool or nail or screw, invariably I could not find it. I would go where I had been sent to look for it, and look and look and finally wait. Soon enough my father would be there with impatient words: "How couldn't you see it? It was right here in front of you!" And it was!

In my dread that precisely this would happen, I could not see. My father's judgment that I was blind and useless only confirmed my belief that I could not see. And then I could not see!

Even my father's presence became something I tried not to feel or be aware of. For a long time I withdrew into fantasies where I was someone else, somewhere else, at some other time. Only when my name was called and I had to answer was I present and then only partially. To this day, when someone impatiently demands that I see, I cannot see. It seems that whatever I am to look for is simply not present. How much blindness comes from this lack of faith?

I have learned a lot about seeing and about presence from this childhood experience. Indeed, I think it is better that I cannot see until I can truly see and until I know I am in the presence of the One whom I am seeing. Because I see this way now, I am not so afraid. My faith in myself has grown, and I am vulnerably present almost all the time. But this is possible not primarily because my faith in myself has been established through much love, but because I have faith in God, in his unseen presence and love.

This in turn has allowed me to love and be present to others. It makes me want to be more and more vulnerable, to be more and more patient with others, to decrease and become like a little child. To be little and full of passion is to have faith, and to be little and share in the passion of Christ is to have faith in him and to love him. How then can I not patiently love everyone else?

Presence is the assurance not only that someone exists but also that he is here. How is Jesus here? In the Holy Spirit, in whom we can do even greater things than the Son himself did, and in the Eucharist! Presence is a matter not only of what or whom we see but also of the unseen. This is a presence that can be absolutely transparent and more real than what we see in the usual ways.

In giving the apostles his Body and Blood at the Last Supper, Jesus said, "This is my body which is for you. Do this in remembrance of me.... This cup is the new covenant in my blood. Do this, as often as you drink it, in remembrance of me" (1 Corinthians 11:24, 25; see Luke 22:19). Is remembrance real presence, or is it only remembered presence?

Consider the crucified thief who asked Jesus if he would *remember* him when he came into his kingdom. Jesus did not simply say that he would remember him or think of him but rather, "Truly, I say to you, *today you will be with me* in Paradise" (Luke 23:43, italics mine).

In the same way, when Jesus said, "Do this in remembrance of me," he meant, "When you do this, *I will be with you!*" That is presence, spoken in the face of death. It is unseen but yet deep and full, totally vulnerable and totally transparent, totally patient and totally passionate, more powerful and more real than the ordinary presence of which the eyes can assure us.

The Pharisee who prayed in the temple loomed large, at least in his own eyes and estimation, while he told the Lord all the things he had done. The publican, who knew he was indeed a sinner, who knew he could never do enough, decreased before the Lord, asking for mercy. He kept his eyes down, not only in repentance and not only looking into himself, but also probably looking more deeply into the unfathomable mystery of the Lord whose mercy he sought and surely received. It is he who went away justified (see Luke 18:10–14).

If I want to create a powerful presence of my own, that presence may leave no room for the presence of God or of anyone else. Adoration, worship, praise and thanksgiving allow me to know the presence of God. Each of these dispositions reaches out into the unseen and is willing to decrease, to become little enough to adore, to worship, to truly give thanks. 🙠

CHAPTER SIX

FAITH AND PASSIONATE GIVING

Sell all that you have and distribute to the poor, and you will have treasure in heaven; and come, follow me" (Luke 18:22).

When Jesus searched for faith among those whom he met, he looked for more than whether they believed he had the power to perform miracles. Jesus wanted people to recognize him and to meet him with faith. This faith engages, involves participation and draws one to enter into the power of Jesus' own self-giving love.

God *is* self-giving love, and the Son became human to share this with all so that all creation will become the kingdom of God. We who are made in his image and likeness have a particular capacity to love in this way. Indeed, this love, decreasing so as to love in his passion, is the only true human happiness.

As Jesus made his rounds, often those who came forward pleading for help did not fully recognize the need for repentance as their deepest need. Jesus called them all to surrender to him, sometimes even asking them to leave everything to follow him. Ultimately this surrender to Jesus Christ requires passion, and surrender in turn yields the passion to be able to give oneself as Jesus himself has done.

Give Them Something to Eat!

If we look more deeply into the signs and wonders Jesus worked, we see this call to passion and surrender. I see it most clearly in the miraculous multiplication of the loaves and fishes (see Luke 9:12–17).

Note well the apostles' approach to the dilemma of the hungry crowd far from home late in the day: send them away! Do we ever resort to purely natural solutions in ways that foreclose faith? A contemporary ecclesiastical solution to this dilemma might involve the disciples' resolve to form a strategic planning committee so that such an embarrassing situation would never happen again.

The disciples, like us when we want to, have a great capacity to see the obvious: The crowds have nothing to eat. The response of Jesus tells us what faith entails: "*You* give them something to eat" (Luke 9:13, italics mine).

Faith involves us in the passion of Christ for those who are hungry. It does not remain cognitive or intentional but becomes concrete. The spiritual hunger of the crowd is deeper than its physical hunger, and the desire to satisfy this spiritual hunger is why they have remained so long without food for the body. *We* must act in faith together with Jesus to satisfy this need for spiritual and physical food, not because he can't do it without us but because he wants us to participate. Even in becoming flesh, the eternal Word was born of a woman (see Galatians 4:4) rather than simply dropping out of the heavens. Again, he wanted a most privileged one of *us* to participate!

Is it any surprise that, among all those people who have gathered to listen to the words of Jesus, the one who does have a small amount of food is a child (see John 6:9)? Similarly, Jesus instructs his disciples to have the crowd sit on the ground, like children at a picnic.

After he has blessed the little food they have, it is his disciples who must distribute it. Imagine the trepidation you would feel in their place, knowing that you will run out of the little bit of food you have to distribute before you get to the end of the first row! The disciples discovered an important truth for us all: If we let Jesus bless and break the little we think we have, and if in our vulnerability we give all of the little we think we have, we will never run out. In fact, we will have more left over than we started with! Thus faith becomes explicit and concrete.

If we are careful never to allow ourselves to get stuck in such a tight spot, relying always on our own calculations and provisions, how will we ever know what faith and true peace are? A priest serving in the Holy Land was able to obtain a great deal of rice, and he decided to give it to a very poor woman so that she would not have to worry each day where the next meal for her and her children was coming from. But the woman refused the gift outright, saying, "If I accept this, how will I be able to receive each day my daily bread?"

God gave the Israelites in the desert manna and later quail every single day. But if the Israelites tried to take more than their daily bread, what they tried to save became infested with worms and rotted (see Exodus 16:20). Accumulating goods can lead to covetousness. Then, just as King David's lust consumed Bathsheba, Uriah's little lamb of a wife (see 2 Samuel 12:1–6), so we too can become enslaved in craving the little we do not have.

Beyond the Material

We need this faith, but not only regarding food and material possessions. This was the mistake of the crowds who sought to make Jesus king after his multiplication of the loaves and fishes. They did not understand the sign. They probably thought that with a king like this, there would never be famine again!

Mother Teresa pointed out that she saw the greatest poverty in the first-world nations, where many are well fed. Most precious for many of us is our time, our space and our love. We can become grasping with these gifts that could be shared so profitably with those who need them. Indeed, it is the way I use or abuse such gifts that decides how I live and how I die.

Do I feel that I am always running out of time? Do I have a desperate need to find my personal space and quality time? How often time grasped in this way turns out to be lonely and empty! On the other hand, if we take the little we think we have, let the Lord bless it and in total vulnerability give ourselves to those in need, especially the least ones, we will never run out.

This is the faith Jesus looks for, not simply a belief that he can perform miracles but faith that joins us in his total giving of himself. We must give as lavishly as he has given to us: our time, our money, the very presence of Jesus, his Body and Blood. It is not enough to admire and ponder such generous love and faith in others; rather, we must exercise our faith with passion.

By realizing that we are all poor, that we are all in the lowest place, we will become humble and childlike enough to do really great things. The greatest thing of all is to love as Christ has loved us, to love in his love.

Nothing to Lose

We are to be perfect as our heavenly Father is perfect (see Matthew 5:48). But how can we expect to actually give *everything*? We are not infinite like God!

Indeed, we can only give what we have and are able to give. But one implication about giving everything is that we must accept God's will in everything, whatever comes. I can dispose myself to give whatever I can, whatever I have, with no reservation. If there is anything I have decided in advance I will *not* give, this is surely the first area for me to open before the Lord in prayer.

God is not a sadist but rather a lover. He does not take things from us to punish us or make us unhappy. Rather he wants to take away the unhappiness caused by clinging and refusing to let go. So I must never say, "I will give up everything *but…*"

A religious sister who had been coming to me for some time for spiritual direction was always very anxious about what the future would bring. She seemed particularly concerned that her provincial might transfer her to another mission. She tried to free herself from this anxiety and finally felt she had. But when I gave her the penance in the sacrament of reconciliation to simply go before the Lord and offer him everything, she cried out, "I can't do that! What if he lets me be transferred?"

If it isn't fear over an assignment, it will be something else. I sometimes invite a person who has come to see me for spiritual direction or therapy to start with the most difficult thing to talk about, the matter he or she is least inclined to speak of. I do not do this to corner or embarrass the person but to free him or her to speak. (I never use this approach when I feel that the person might react defensively. The littler I am and the more aware of my poverty, the more likely I am to know when to suggest such things, when to speak and when to be silent.)

Saint Francis, after he had left father and home, given his clothes to a beggar and set out to live in poverty and abandonment to Christ, was struggling one day over his revulsion against lepers. He felt his dread of them was a sign that he had not totally entrusted himself to Christ. Then what did he hear but the little bell lepers were required to ring wherever they went to warn people to stay away from them!

Shaking with dread but bursting with love, Saint Francis ran down the road to embrace the approaching leper and to exchange clothes with him. Rejoicing as he went on his way, he turned back to once more salute the leper but found that he had vanished. Vulnerability meeting and embracing vulnerability turns into transparency embracing transparency, and so the poor in spirit find Christ.

This is, of course, simply being open to the Spirit. We can receive the Spirit, who is divine Gift and Love in person and thus totally transparent, only when we allow *ourselves* to be transformed into gift. We cannot measure this gift, because how then could we receive the unlimited gift of the Holy Spirit, of grace, of a share in God's own infinite life? The only way to give ourselves completely is to give ourselves over and over again, to die daily, to take up our cross daily (see Luke 9:23) and to offer ourselves completely, whatever that will mean today.

This is a yoke that is easy (see Matthew 11:28–30) compared to the yoke of self-centeredness, the yoke of worry and trying to control everything. What is there to lose in losing self-sufficiency? My fear that it will be taken from me makes me lose it anyway!

To take up my cross daily is to lay down the yoke of self and to take up the yoke of self-giving love, following Jesus as he carries his cross, summoning the passion of my whole life in his passion. Such faith and such passion defy analysis; we can only understand them as we live in God with all our heart, living in his passion.

Our life, the lives of others, our world, are then viewed with a faith that is a passionate patience, a gift from God through our sharing in the passion of his Son. Pope Benedict XVI described this faith in the patience of God as he officially began his reign:

> How often we wish that God would show himself stronger, that he would strike decisively, defeating evil and creating a better world. All ideologies of power justify themselves in exactly this way; they justify the destruction of whatever would stand in the way of progress and the liberation of humanity. We suffer on account of God's patience. And yet we need his patience. God, who became a lamb, tells us that the world is

saved by the Crucified One, not by those who crucified him. The world is redeemed by the patience of God. It is destroyed by the impatience of man.[1]

We see the patience of the Shepherd in his becoming one of the sheep, the Lamb who is sacrificed out of love for all the rest. This is why the title of this book is *The Passion of the Lamb.*

CHAPTER SEVEN

THE PASSION OF THE TRINITY

God has sent the Spirit of his Son into our hearts, crying, 'Abba, Father!'" (Galatians 4:6).

The story goes that Saint Augustine was walking along the shore, trying to understand how it is possible for there to be three Persons in one God. He saw a little boy digging in the sand with a seashell and asked him what he was doing. The little boy said that he was digging a hole deep enough to put the whole ocean in.

Saint Augustine responded that it would never be possible to dig a hole deep enough to put the whole ocean inside. Then the little boy, presumably the Christ child, answered, "It would be easier for me to do that than for you to fit the mystery of the Trinity into your mind."

Infinite Love

How do we know God if he is unseen, if he is greater than what we can understand? Attempts made over the ages to help make the Trinity comprehensible—shamrocks, diagrams, theological analogies—go only so far. Perhaps the problem is too exclusive a reliance upon the mind, whereas it might be more fruitful to start from the heart. Heart, mind, imagination: all the faculties come together to help us understand the mystery of the Trinity. But perhaps the best starting point is to look at the Trinity as the mystery of God's unlimited self-giving love.

God is unseen, and yet he has let us see him in the Person of the Son who became human, whom "we have looked upon and touched with our hands" (1 John 1:1). Jesus Christ told us that he is the eternal Son of his beloved Father, *Abba*. In turn, this Father called Jesus his beloved Son at his baptism and at his transfiguration.

Before ascending to the Father, Jesus promised that the Paraclete would come to us and dwell in us. This is the Holy Spirit, through whom Jesus was conceived in the womb of Mary, the Mother of God, and who also was manifest at the moment of Jesus' baptism. God himself revealed all this to us!

Often when people think about God, they think first of his power, his omnipotence. God indeed is impassible, self-contained and perfect. He is complete in himself and never deficient or weak in any way. Nothing can touch him. Yet we have to reconcile all of the "omni" attributes of God—his omnipotence (being all-powerful, almighty), his omniscience (being all-knowing), his omnipresence (being all-present)—with his being all-loving. Indeed, of all the wonderful things we can say of this one God in three Persons, the most striking is the outpouring love among them. Their love is infinite, without limit.

In our times, maybe more than ever, we need to really understand that "God is love" (1 John 4:16). Surely we must understand this if we are to understand our own love, passion and desire.

While holding to all the truth of God's unchanging, infinite perfection, can we also recognize that he is perfect in being totally, infinitely self-emptying, that God is love as infinite self-gift? If so, maybe we can speak of the attribute of God as omni-kenotic (all self-emptying)!

Can we go on from there to speak about how God is omni-vulnerable, omni-patient, omni-transparent, omni-passionate? Then we might better understand how being little lets God live in us. He loves us with self-giving love, which is the perfection of the very qualities we have been speaking of as necessary to enter his kingdom. He has become little himself to reveal this to us!

Maybe we can better understand what otherwise could seem to be a riddle or some useless piece of dogmatic baggage: that we believe in the Trinity! Each of the three is a divine Person precisely insofar as each one—Father, Son and Holy Spirit—infinitely gives himself to the other divine Persons in love in the way appropriate to their relationship. Thus we can begin to see how the intercommunion of self-giving love among them is so perfect that they are one God. By infinitely giving himself, each divine Person is perfectly the Person he is.

Loving in the Image of God

God made us in his image and likeness, and so we are like the Trinity. We see this in our longing for love and our desire to become one with those whom we love, though we experience these things in limitation and even in deficiency. Think of the main theme of the songs we compose, the poems we write, the stories we tell. Is it not love, the longing and yearning to find perfect union in love?

The Trinity is an excellent model for our love as human beings. What is it, after all, to be a human person? (After a generation of personalistic philosophy and psychology, we should by now be able to answer that question!) To be a human person is to be capable of being in relationship with other persons and to deeply long for that personal relationship.

In the theological language the church adopted to speak of God, the word *person* (*prosupon, hypostasis*) did not have all the psychological meaning we now give to the word. It meant more simply "an individual being or substance." Divine Persons are self-subsisting or self-grounding, whereas created persons like us subsist in and have been created by God. What human persons and divine Persons have in common is that we are subjects, and both human and divine subjects are "intersubjective" or interpersonal. Each of the three divine Persons is perfect in himself and in the perfect oneness of God, whereas human persons are constituted as persons only in relationship with God.

In his theology of the body, Pope John Paul II calls this our "original solitude." Each one of us dwells, as did that first human being, alone before God as is no other creature, even after woman was taken from that man's side (see Genesis 2). Inspired by the revelation found in the Book of Genesis, Pope John Paul therefore defines our humanness as consisting most especially in our "nuptial capacity." Created in the image and likeness of God, we have the ability to make a free and total gift of ourselves.[1]

The word *nuptial* means "having to do with marriage." It indicates the way a man and a woman share themselves totally with each other, becoming one flesh. Thus our "bodiliness" and our sexuality are essential to our humanity.

As in all our language about God, we are speaking analogously when we talk of how God loves us this way, not because God's way of loving is not really like our way of loving but because it is *more* real, infinitely real. Our human capacity to love deeply, in marriage and in other self-giving relationships as well, is our best way of beginning to understand what it must be for God to love. From our experience of our own personhood, we can start to realize what a divine Person might be like and how that Person might love.

Each of the three divine Persons, as revealed in sacred Scripture, loves the other divine Persons in infinite, limitless self-gift. The Father eternally begets the Son, the Son eternally loves the Father in filial obedience, and the Holy Spirit is the love flow-

ing between the Father and the Son, Love bearing fruit that is
Love in Person.

Our own experiences of never running out of love—the love
a parent feels for even a wayward child, for example—reflect the
self-emptying love of the three divine Persons, who are *infinitely*
self-emptying but never empty. There is no loss of perfection in
this emptying; the perfection of God is that *God is love!*

As we are made in the image and likeness of God (see
Genesis 1:26), self-gift is the means to direct our whole lives in the
most fully human way, with all our desire and passion, toward
God. Moreover, the Trinity is not a detached intercommunion of
love. Rather God's love flows freely outside of himself into his
creation and eventually into his Incarnation and into the sancti-
fication and salvation of all creation.

In the image and likeness of God's fruitful love, a man and a
woman can love in a way that bears the fruit of new human life!
Loving relationships outside the conjugal love of a man and a
woman likewise bear fruit appropriate to their familial or friend-
ship bonds. The more our human, personal love shares in divine
love, the more fruitful this love is.

Grace: The Free Gift

Jesus shows us that the kingdom of God has nothing to do with
worldly power or domination. If he had not revealed something
quite different, we could be left hopeless of ever entering that
kingdom. But the Good News is that to enter into the kingdom of
God requires becoming small. That fact makes the kingdom of
heaven accessible to all.

Still, there is no way in which we can enter the kingdom of
God on our own. We must instead receive it as a gift the beloved
Father gives to his little children. In other words, it is all grace. It
is free!

Our beloved Father has given us his beloved Son as our means to enter the kingdom. He gives this gift not dispassionately but through the Incarnation and passion of the Son and the self-emptying gift of the Holy Spirit.

What this means is that grace is not simply any gift but rather the gift through which God shares his very life with us! This life of God in us is called supernatural insofar as we could never reach it by our own natural means. It comes from beyond our nature, from God, to crown and complete what is natural to us as human beings. This is the meaning of the doctrine that grace builds upon nature, just as two human persons can bring much to each other that neither could have achieved on his or her own.

All our language about God is analogous: We use our limited human understanding and experience to describe the unlimited and infinite. To say that God is not dispassionate does not mean that he has passions in exactly the same way we humans do; rather it means that God is no stranger to our passion. How could he be, since he created us?

Our human passions are heavily dominated by our bodiliness and are subject to the many vicissitudes of our lives. Our bodiliness is a uniquely human way in which we are able to be present and to share ourselves in love. Our intellect can direct our passion, which is influenced by our bodiliness, to freely seek God with the help of his grace and revelation. Then we can lead lives of love, in which the limitations of our natural humanness are stretched supernaturally by grace into the infinite love of God. Grace is a sharing in God's own life, gifting us with forgiveness, salvation and redemption through the Incarnation of the eternal Son.

Now the self-emptying love of the Son in his Incarnation begins to make a lot more sense in terms of how we know God loves. Each of the three divine Persons loves in an infinite, unlimited self-gift. This love pours out from God into creation and, in a most intimately personal way, into the lives of human beings created in the image and likeness of God.

Then the eternal Son brings the love of God even more intimately to us by becoming one of us. This is a revelation to us of the way God loves: the infinitely outpouring love of the Father who eternally begets the Son now *sends* the Son for *our* salvation. The Son becomes flesh, becomes human, becomes *one of us* as an expression in history of his eternal, filial, loving obedience to his Father. We will discuss this fleshed-out expression of God's love in the next chapter.

CHAPTER EIGHT

JESUS CHRIST: THE DIVINE
BECOMES HUMAN

For God so loved the world that he gave his only Son"
(John 3:16).

The Incarnation of the Son of God is the most unmistakable
revelation to us of how God loves. An adequate summary of the
church's faith in Jesus Christ is that he is the eternal divine Son,
an eternal divine Person with a divine nature, who at a particular
point in time took on a human nature. These truths are all proclaimed not only in sacred Scripture, inspired by the Holy Spirit
in an absolutely unique way that is normative for all further
unfolding of the faith, but also in the church's tradition, which
with Scripture make up the "deposit of faith."

Though logically we should begin with a detailed study of
what the New Testament says about who Jesus is, we will look first
at the later doctrinal formulations of the church and then turn to
the Scriptures, hoping thus to show how the church's doctrine
fully reflects what is proclaimed about Jesus Christ in the inspired
words of Scripture.

Living Tradition

In the centuries after the death of the original witnesses, the writings of the Fathers of the church amplified the teaching about

Jesus Christ, grounded in the revealed faith recorded in sacred Scripture. They formulated this doctrine into creeds, which included also the teaching of the earliest ecumenical councils.

The use of the word *ecumenical* here does not mean "interfaith dialogue" but refers to those councils that convened bishops representing the whole church, East and West. Their most solemn definitions are accepted as unchanging doctrine, part of the faith and tradition of the church. Here are some of the more important truths about Jesus Christ defined by these early councils.

The Council of Ephesus in 431 solemnly declared Mary to be the Mother of God, a feast the church celebrates on January 1. This title tells us that Mary did not merely give birth to the humanity of Jesus but conceived and gave birth to the whole Person Jesus Christ, the eternal Son of God. If one asks how a woman could conceive and give birth to the Son of God, the answer has to be, as Scripture says, through the power of the Holy Spirit (see Luke 1:35)! Saint Cyril (375–444), patriarch of Alexandria, formulated this title Mother of God in his teaching against Nestorius (d. 451), patriarch of Constantinople.[1]

We should appreciate the fact that what could seem to us to be abstract theology was so important to Christians of the fifth century that they took to the streets to defend Mary under this title. They would not give in to those who sought to diminish her role as mother by seeing her as contributing simply a humanity for Christ. It is also interesting to note that, long before the divisions of the eleventh and sixteenth centuries, the universal church gave Mary this title of honor for her role in the Incarnation. So devotion that singles out Mary's unique role in salvation surely is not just a "Catholic thing"!

In what way is Jesus divine, and in what way is he human? Even before the Council of Ephesus met, the first Council of Nicea in 325 had declared that Jesus Christ is divine in every way that the Father is divine. Namely, he is consubstantial, *homo-ousios*, "of the same divine being or nature" as the Father. This first of the ecumenical councils formulated this doctrine using the teaching of Saint Athanasius (296–373), patriarch of Alexandria, against the priest Arius (d. 336), whose followers are reputed to have diminished the full divinity of the Son by the slogan "There was a time when he was not!"[2]

Then the great Council of Chalcedon in 451 insisted that Jesus Christ is human in every way that we are human, except sin, and divine in every way that the Father is divine.[3] This is called the hypostatic union, meaning that Jesus Christ is the union in one Person (or *hypostasis*) of two natures, one human and one divine.[4]

It is true, of course, that in the New Testament Jesus nowhere refers to himself as "the hypostatic union"! *Hypostasis* is a word drawn from the philosophical vocabulary of the fifth century to try to say what "person" is and how the humanity and divinity in Jesus could come together in one person or *hypostasis*.

Other councils, chiefly three held at Constantinople from the fourth to the seventh centuries, further refined this core teaching of the church about Jesus. The First Council of Constantinople in 381 defended the true humanity and divinity of Jesus against tendencies to diminish the fullness of either, as Apollinaris (310–390) did in saying that the humanity of Jesus did not need to have a human soul since the eternal Word could fulfill that function.[5] In 553 the Second Council of Constantinople taught that the one person with a human and divine nature is a *divine* Person, not a human person or personality. The Person of the Son of God, eternally divine in nature, at the Incarnation assumed a human nature as well, remaining a divine Person.[6]

Finally, the Third Council of Constantinople in 681 taught against the Monothelites. The latter did not think Jesus Christ had a human will, since this would conflict with his divine will. But if Jesus did not have a human will, how can we understand his human freedom?[7]

True God and True Man

How did these council doctrines find their way into the life of believers? The Council of Nicea formulated a creed reflecting the church's faith regarding Christ, which the Council of Chalcedon reaffirmed with some addenda. This is the creed we profess at Mass every Sunday and solemnity. It is good to meditate on each article of the creed, since each phrase embodies a clear teaching formulated only after long debate and with a careful selection of words.

Many people have negative ideas about doctrine and dogma, as if the church is trying to say too much, to tell people how to think. In fact, the solemn definition of doctrine happens slowly, often over centuries. And dogma is mainly concerned with setting the parameters, the boundaries, what has to be included and what cannot be excluded, not necessarily claiming to explain everything. Notice in these examples of doctrine about Christ that the church never tried to spell out exactly *how* a human soul goes together with the eternal Word or *how* a human free will and a divine will coalesce in the one Person of Christ.

Most of the heresies over the years arose from attempts to simplify the understanding of who Jesus is. For example, either he is truly divine and then somehow not exactly human (monophysitism or docetism), or he is truly human and somehow adopted into a divine sonship or status (adoptionism). The fullness of the Catholic faith always involves a "both and," not an "either or." Jesus is a divine Person who is *both* divine *and* human; God is *both* one God *and* three divine Persons.

The process can sound cosmic, not personal or passionate.

How does any of this have to do with being last, least, like a little child?

Precisely in this: the eternal Son of God, equal to the Father in his divinity, became human by being born as a little child. The witness of his life is the first profound and unmistakable revelation of the unique way to God. In revealing himself to us, God did not choose a mighty theophany, some unavoidable vision for the whole world to see, some unmistakably divine manifestation of power. As God spoke to Elijah on Mount Horeb not in the rushing wind or the great storm but in a whisper (see 1 Kings 19), so God reveals himself to us in the carpenter of Nazareth who had "nowhere to lay his head" (Matthew 8:20; Luke 9:58).

To diminish either the true divinity or the humanity of Christ is to lose the fullness of the mystery of God's love in Christ. Either God did not really go so far to become close to us, or it was not really God who became human but just another prophet.

Think about it. If you want to express your love or to help someone you love, you could send a letter or email of support, you could even send someone to convey your love, or you could go in person to the loved one. The faith of the church is that God has done the last of these possibilities. Jesus Christ is the Son of God in *Person;* he has truly become one of us. He loves us that much!

Questions About Jesus Today

We have not gone into detail about all the problems of vocabulary and language in these doctrinal definitions. Besides the problems of terminology between the Latin West and the Greek East, some of the terms were used in different senses at different times. One might wonder, as did reformers who broke from the church, how legitimate it is to adopt later, more philosophical language to say who Jesus is. Are such language and the theology behind it faithful to the earliest witnesses, or are they developments quite different from what the earliest Christians believed?

In our times the question arises again, opening up some controversial areas of research on Jesus. Every Christmas and Easter there are news magazines and television networks that run sensationalist specials on the "new" research on Jesus, especially the infamous Jesus Seminar.[8] In fact, there is very little new about the doubts being expressed and the questions being asked. Such theories and plots have been proposed over the centuries to discredit the claims of Christianity. The force of this research can have serious effects, generating a great deal of confusion and skepticism about what we really know about who Jesus is and what he taught. Such "scholarship" is often marginal, though its proponents know how to use the media and are often good at getting in front of a camera.

The upshot is a very minimalist sense of how much in the New Testament really goes back to Jesus. Dan Brown's *The Da Vinci Code* is only one of the more recent examples of popular writing that goes even beyond this research, mixing fiction into some historical study and confusing popular minds, which are prone to confusion anyway.

As we suggested earlier, some much more solid biblical scholarship, including some Catholic biblical scholarship, is also somewhat minimalist in what it admits as historical in the New Testament, leaving the believer with the overall impression that we really don't have much to go on. Such research creates a gap between the residue of what biblical scholars consider reliable and the rest of tradition, sending the clear message that unless we can show incontrovertibly that something is in the Scriptures, it is an illegitimate development and not a solid foundation for faith. We are left with more questions than answers.

There surely are many motives for these studies, including a genuine wish to purify our faith and our understanding of Jesus in light of new data such as the Dead Sea Scrolls and the Gnostic gospels. The Catholic church, through papal teaching and through the guidelines proposed by the Pontifical Biblical Commission, rightly insists upon the necessity of the historical-critical method in studying sacred Scripture and the helpfulness of such tools. Sometimes, however, it seems that exegetes and biblical scholars, endowing themselves with a dogmatic authority they would resist if exercised by the Magisterium, treat hypotheses as dogma and dismiss any theological or spiritual meaning accorded to Scripture. They thereby have created a lot of unnecessary resistance to their work.

But there sometimes is more going on and more damage done, and we should not underestimate the sometimes thinly disguised desire to cut Jesus and the church down to size, to make them over in someone's image and likeness, according to that person's agenda. The arbitrariness of the presuppositions used and the conclusions drawn by such groups as the Jesus Seminar and the liberation and feminist theologies should make us suspicious. Sheep follow easily, especially if there is a sensationalistic appeal or story line and a popular presentation.

Who Do You Say That I Am?

The real Jesus continues to loom above this Tower of Babel with all its ignorant talk about him. It seems to me that Mel Gibson gave us Jesus unbound, so to speak. We also can learn much by looking to the faith of the ages, expressed in theology, art, architecture and perhaps especially in the lives and writings of the saints and mystics.

The New Testament reflects the uniquely inspired earliest testimonies of faith in Jesus Christ, normative for all faith in him, and there especially the real Jesus emerges. If we enter into this faith and express it in a life of self-giving love, being sure to center on the Eucharist and self-emptying prayer, we easily can separate the wheat from the chaff and recognize when some supposed scholar is offering stones for us to eat instead of bread.

I want to focus particularly on the titles with which Jesus is named because I find in them a condensed theology born of the earliest faith in Jesus and in his proclamation of the kingdom. Moreover, I have noted a marvelous convergence in the dogmatic faith of the earliest doctrine about Jesus formulated in the ecumenical councils, beginning in the fourth century, and the faith in Jesus reflected in the scriptural titles for him. Note that some of the contemporary "Jesus research" applies the same empty reasoning to these titles as it does to his words and actions reported in Scripture, and often not much is left afterward.

LORD

One of the earliest ways of proclaiming faith in Jesus Christ was by saying, "Jesus is Lord!" Indeed, this seems to have been the profession of faith most common in the early church.

What does *Lord* mean here? *Kurios* in Greek, the word is at once a translation of the Hebrew name for God, *Yahweh*, which could not be written, and also a title to honor a human being as lord and master. Both a divine and a human meaning for the same word! I propose that the earliest faith of the church began to draw upon the double meaning of the title "Lord" to profess faith in Jesus as more than just a human master but also God (see 1 Corinthians 11:26; 16:22; Philippians 2: 9–11; Revelation 22:20).

The earliest followers of Christ were, of course, Jews. In their solid monotheistic faith in one God, it would have been inconceivable that the Jesus who called God his Father would also be God! Yet they had to come to grips with the fact that he went about forgiving sins, something only God can do (see

Mark 2:1–12). And what about the unusual intimacy that he claimed with God in calling him *Abba* and inviting others to do so (see Matthew 6:9, 32; 23:9; Romans 8:14–17; Galatians 4:6)?

This wonderworker also reinterpreted the law and the Sabbath, clearly claiming a divine authority over these. Indeed, it was this very behavior that led to the charge of blasphemy, the one valid bit of testimony his accusers had against him. If he was not the divine Son of God but only human, he surely was blaspheming!

Whether Jesus was called Lord in this double sense during his lifetime and before his Resurrection is unclear. But no matter when this began, the title clearly condenses the truth that the ecumenical councils eventually summarized: that he is at once divine and human. Before that kind of language could be used, this title "Lord" professed that same faith.

Son of God

The title "Son of God" also had a broad usage. It could be applied to Israel as a nation, to angels or to anyone who was singularly under the power of or who bore the authority of God. We see these human meanings clearly being stretched in those places in the New Testament where Jesus is called not simply *a* son of God but *the* Son of God. This title once again bears the double meaning, human and divine. Its use professes faith in who Jesus is and thus brings us to a fuller understanding of the kingdom of God Jesus proclaimed.

It is of critical importance to remember that we mean "divine" in the unique way in which Jesus revealed what God is like and how he loves. Surely, already in the history of Israel God showed himself willing to have mercy upon and to relate intimately with his people. Particularly the writings of the prophets reveal this intimate love. Yet Jesus went a quantum leap beyond anything revealed about God up to that point. The divinity of Christ, as church doctrine eventually asserted, is not a divinity of Greek or Roman philosophical conception but that of the God of Abraham, Isaac and Jacob. This God fulfilled the promise of the ages by sending his Son.

In whatever sense the meaning of these titles may have developed after the Resurrection, such development must be seen as completely legitimate and shining from the light of the faith that Jesus already summoned during his earthly ministry, by what he did even more than by what he said or what he was called.

Often the more explicit claims to divinity found in the Gospel of John are rejected as a later theology out of harmony with the other three Gospels and going beyond them. For example, Jesus' saying, "Before Abraham was, I am" (John 8:58) marks a clear identification with God's words to Moses from the burning bush (see Exodus 3:6, 14; Deuteronomy 32:39; Isaiah 43:10). Similarly, Jesus says of the ultimate expression of his passion in terms of his eternal sonship, when he will be lifted high on the cross, "Then you will know that I am he" (John 8:28).

I am inclined to believe that the core of this Gospel was written much earlier than is usually assumed and that it reflects a fairly complete self-revelation of Jesus to those most intimate to him, including his most beloved disciple. The church has always believed that all these Scriptures are inspired; moreover, the Pontifical Biblical Commission has reminded us that it is wrong to layer the value of certain Scriptures because of the hypothesized age or authorship.[9] A canonical approach to Scripture is better; this takes Scripture as a whole and lets it speak as a whole.[10]

The Suffering Son of Man

Even minimalist Scripture scholars accept the fact that Jesus used the title Son of Man (see Daniel 7:13–14) to describe himself, probably in conjunction with some of the meaning given to the mysterious suffering servant in Isaiah 53. Indeed, Son of Man is the only title we find Jesus himself using to describe himself (see Mark 10:45, for example). In doing so, Jesus clearly reinterpreted any of the meanings in Scripture or current in his time about the identity of the Messiah. The Savior is the suffering Son of Man, who is to come on the clouds of heaven and who gains his victory by giving himself for all.

Perhaps Jesus silenced those who recognized his true identity as Messiah (translated into Greek as *Christ*, meaning "the anointed one") precisely because he knew that the many interpretations others would give to this title would be political ones. All these understandings he unequivocally rejected in favor of the true meaning of his divine sonship. He would come as a lowly one, and he would suffer and die for all. His victory would lie in his apparent defeat, in his self-gift.

In Daniel 7:13–14 the "one like a son of man," who comes on the clouds of heaven, really seems to refer to the whole nation of Israel. So also in Ezekiel 37, where God addresses the prophet as "son of man," it is the whole nation that rises from the dry bones. Jesus indeed takes this meaning into his person, for he *is* the entire people of God in that they are members of his body.

There were those in the time of Jesus who believed in the Resurrection but who understood it in light of Ezekiel and Daniel, where the whole nation would rise at once. Jesus rose from the dead bodily but alone, and in his body we too will rise as a mighty people of God on the last day.

It is this "alone" of Jesus that gives us the key to who he is. Even in drawing upon the Scriptures, Jesus reinterpreted these in a new way. He often said, "Truly, I say to you" (see for example Matthew 10:15; Mark 9:1; John 12:24), in contrast to the prophets' "The word of the Lord came to me." He positioned

himself with the authority to make a radical kingdom proclamation and to further claim that access to the kingdom could only
come through him.

The title "Son of Man" thus has a double meaning: it includes
the whole nation of human persons raised up by God as well as
the divine Son, the firstborn of many brothers and sisters, in
whom we are adopted. Jesus is not simply the first one to walk
this way of salvation. Indeed, he *is* the Way (see John 14:6).

The Scandal

We have mentioned that Jesus shunned titles such as "the
Messiah," which were associated with many notions of worldly
power, because he feared they would be misunderstood. Yet he
accepted Saint Peter's profession of faith in him as Messiah, "You
are the Christ, the Son of the living God" (Matthew 16:16),
because he knew Peter made it in faith: "Blessed are you, Simon
Bar-Jona! For flesh and blood has not revealed this to you, but my
Father who is in heaven" (Matthew 16:17). Perhaps the way Jesus
reinterpreted all these titles, all these promises to Israel, can be
found best in the ancient hymn Saint Paul quoted in his Letter to
the Philippians:

> Christ Jesus...though he was in the form of God, did not
> count equality with God a thing to be grasped but emptied
> himself, taking the form of a servant, being born in the like-
> ness of men. And being found in human form he humbled
> himself and became obedient unto death, even death on a
> cross. Therefore God has highly exalted him and bestowed on
> him the name which is above every name, that at the name of
> Jesus every knee should bow, in heaven and on earth and
> under the earth, and every tongue confess that Jesus Christ is
> Lord, to the glory of God the Father. (Philippians 2:5–11)

The acclamation at the end is taken from Isaiah 45:23 and is addressed there to Yahweh, God: "To me every knee shall bow, every tongue shall swear." Here Paul is clearly calling Jesus the Lord and Christ (the Messiah) in the way that Yahweh is God, and this confession arises in praise of Jesus' self-emptying love!

Paul probably took this hymn from an already common liturgical profession of the lordship of Jesus. Even this seemingly clear proclamation of faith in the eternal One who empties himself has been a point of controversy among some biblical scholars. These suggest that there is no hint of the preexistence or divinity of Jesus in this hymn, but that it is only talking about Jesus as the new Adam, who unlike the first Adam did not grasp at equality with God. Yet there is clearly much more than a new Adam understanding of Jesus here.

There always seems to be that urge to doubt, to diminish the power of who Jesus is. We should not be surprised that the reality of who Jesus is remains a scandal, a stumbling block, for many who hold back from believing. To them it seems like a fairy tale, but the proclamation "Jesus is Lord" has a power beyond any fairy tale, myth or legend. The power lies in the person of Jesus Christ.

Indeed, all analysis becomes abstract and dry, perhaps skeptical and minimalist, before the person of Jesus Christ. Even the critics who dismiss him often seem to spend the rest of their lives studying him and trying to argue why they continue to dismiss him. They too are somehow under his power, a power that has the persuasiveness only love can have.

Perhaps in the end the problems we have in believing and knowing who Jesus is are of this deeper sort, especially for those whose study and experience have made them strangers to childlike faith. It seems unbelievable, just too good to be true, that Jesus is Lord, that he is human like us and at the same time truly

God in person. To believe this is not so much a contradiction as a paradox, as is our faith in God as One and Three.

But the logical difficulties are probably the least problematic. What bothers us more is the vulnerability, the intimacy, the passion. We struggle to really believe that God has not merely spoken his word, that he has not merely sent a prophet, angel or other messenger, but that he has come to us in person, in the Person of the Son. And as if this were not enough, he did not simply drop down out of heaven but entered totally into space and time, into our history and human existence, into our joy and our suffering, into our love and our hope, actually becoming one of us while remaining who he is.

Can we believe that God loves us that much, to truly become incarnate, to truly become human while remaining who he is? Let us become like little children and say, "Yes, Lord, I believe!" ❧

REAL FOOD, REAL DRINK, REAL PRESENCE

"For my flesh is food indeed, and my blood is drink indeed" (John 6:55).

It is disappointing to find out from random surveys that, even among Catholics, there tends to be a rather uninformed if not weak faith about the Eucharist. Much of this is surely due to poor catechesis, but the problem is much deeper. I believe it is a fear of the passion involved in really believing that this concretely is the Body and Blood of Jesus Christ as he told us it is. We are afraid of such realism, because if we begin to accept the Eucharist as real, Jesus will change us profoundly in very explicit and concrete ways.

Some have tried to diminish the reality of the Eucharist by using the word *sign* or *symbol* to explain what Jesus meant when he said, "This is my body,...this is my blood." Some have postulated that Jesus' words "Do this in remembrance of me" (Luke 22:19) point to an understanding of the Eucharist as only a way of signifying what he actually would do later on the cross. The impression is that the Eucharist is not really the Body and Blood of Christ but only points to him. Is he present only in us and in our faith?

The church has found lacking various attempts to describe what happens, what changes through the words of consecration. She has rejected the notions, for example, that the bread and wine remain bread and wine but signify the body and blood of Christ ("transignification") and that the bread and wine remain bread and wine but also become the Body and Blood of Christ ("consubstantiation"). Similarly she has rejected a reduction of the Eucharist to the body and blood of the historical Jesus as he lived on earth ("physicalism"). In reality the Eucharist is the Body and Blood, soul and divinity of the Son of God, now risen and glorified.

"Transubstantiation" is not the only way but perhaps the clearest way to indicate the faith of the church. *Transubstantiation* means "a change of substance but not accidents or appearances." The word *substance* here means "the very being or reality of something." The substance or "real being" of the bread and wine is changed into the very being of the body and blood of Christ, while not the real being but only the appearances of bread and wine remain. Even at the Last Supper Christ's Body and Blood appeared to be bread and wine, though he said, "This is my body,...this is my blood" (Matthew 26:26, 28).

This Aristotelian understanding of reality as made of substance and accidents is alien to our contemporary approach to reality. But it makes the point that, though the substance still looks like bread and wine, it really is the Body and Blood of Christ.

Real Presence

I have come to realize that any tendency to diminish the reality of Christ's presence in the Eucharist usually goes hand in hand with a tendency to diminish the reality of the true humanity or divinity of Jesus in his Incarnation, as well as the importance and reality of the bodily Resurrection. We will demonstrate each of these in due course; here we simply observe the scandal, the stumbling block, which can only be leaped over by love. As with the real and total divinity and humanity of Jesus, the Real Presence is a stumbling block not so much to our minds as to our hearts.

Just about any other solution seems easier to accept than this radically intimate act of love, even the more incredible notion that we have *both* bread and wine *and* the Body and Blood of Jesus. That solution resembles the ideas of Nestorius, who believed that in Jesus Christ we somehow have a human person *and* a divine person. That is one person too many, and it loses the intimacy of our coming together in *one* person with God. It also resembles the idea of the Arians that Christ is divine in some sense but still a creature, or of the adoptionists, who believed Jesus to be a man somehow adopted and made divine.

Just as the church believes that God has come in person in Jesus Christ and that he has truly become human, so the church believes and teaches that the Eucharist truly *is* the Body and Blood of Christ in person. He has become so vulnerable as not only to become incarnate but also to then give us his flesh as real food and his blood as real drink. We must believe and realize this explicitly.

Jesus scandalized his own listeners, as some persons are scandalized today, in describing how concretely he has given himself to us (see John 6:41–66). He has not only become one flesh with us but has given himself—body, blood, soul and divinity, as the Council of Trent (Session 13) solemnly defined—to be eaten and drunk and taken into our own flesh and blood. Now, that is intimacy, that is vulnerability, and that is passion, as concrete, as explicit and as personal as possible.

Jesus said to his apostles and says to us, "Do this in remembrance of me" (Luke 22:19). He uses the word *remember* in a

sense that is close to the Jewish mind and heart, meaning "to participate as intimately as Yahweh's entering into his loving *hesed*
with his people." As I pointed out in chapter 5, the good thief's
request that Jesus *remember* him in his kingdom elicited Jesus'
promise that Dismas would be *with him* that day in paradise (see
Luke 23:39–43). So intimately and personally is Jesus with us
when we celebrate the Eucharist. That is real presence. That is real
intimacy.

Barriers to Eucharistic Intimacy

Earlier I pointed out how hard it is for us to "look upon him
whom [we] have pierced" (John 19:37). It is hard for us to look at
the suffering servant, whose very face accuses us of our infideli-
ties and makes us recognize the evil in our hearts (see Isaiah 53).
Like those self-righteous ones who brought to Jesus the woman
caught in adultery, we look upon his face and find written there
our own sins, exposed not only for ourselves but for everyone to
see (see John 8:3–11).

If the Eucharist truly is the Body and Blood of Christ given
for us, to eat and to drink, then we are exposed as the least ones,
as sinners in need of forgiveness. His self-gift exposes our self-
righteousness. It is easier to keep it a memorial than to realize that
he has gone all the way and given everything, his very life, his very
self. It is easier to ignore the concreteness and make it an abstract
symbol representing something in the past, something that I
walked in on but that does not really involve me. I wasn't really at
Calvary, and he isn't really here in the Eucharist.

Jansenism rears its head from time to time to elicit people's
fear of approaching the sacrament out of a sense of unworthi-
ness. It must be honestly admitted, however, that this is not the
main problem in our times. Much more problematic is the ten-

dency to eat and drink the Body and Blood of Christ unworthily. Many of us come to Communion without fully realizing what we are doing. We come seemingly without preparation, such as confession.

We see in parts of the church a tendency to downplay what is really taking place at the Mass by making the celebration as casual and informal as possible. We fear boredom, and so we make our celebrations so busy with singing and speaking and doing that there is no room to realize concretely the meaning of the Mass. Quiet time is readily allowed following the proclamation of the Word, but quiet thanksgiving after receiving the Eucharist is somehow suspect. Even priests and those living the consecrated life have abandoned many simple practices that allowed their interiority to develop.

Instead of taking time to deepen our relationship with the Lord in the Eucharist, we hurry into the gathering space to socialize. Or worse, we socialize in church, distracting others from prayer. We don't take the opportunity to let the reality sink in, to assimilate him whom we have received.

Is this abuse of the Eucharist similar to the way society approaches sexuality? Recreational sex allows people to avoid the profound vulnerability of making a total gift of self to another person. Do we likewise seek to avoid the vulnerability of eucharistic intimacy with the Lord?

My point here is that the church often does not succeed in helping people to enter into the quiet, into the union, into the conversation with the Lord and with each other that people need. And if people do not find it at Mass, they will look elsewhere.

A friend told me that since her mother's death she had become Wiccan, primarily because this cult includes a feminine goddess but also because through it she can contact her mother ritually and speak to her. I replied that I too speak to her mother in prayer regularly, but I would never dare to manipulate the many spiritual powers we do not understand.

We often see people borrowing practices from Eastern religion and philosophy, such as transcendental meditation, Tai Chi, yoga and a host of other self-help ways to relieve stress.

Many years ago, as a Benedictine novice, I wrote to a Trappist monk who was involved in the dialogue between Christianity and the East that Thomas Merton had begun. I asked him for a bibliography or some way to enter more deeply into methods of Eastern prayer. He wrote back that this dialogue has indeed been rich for both parties, but that all I needed could be found within my Christian tradition. He suggested that I simply read *The Cloud of Unknowing,* a spiritual classic from the fourteenth century. I did, and it changed my life and prayer. It convinced me that what I need is right under my nose.

Devotion tries to restore a sense of what is holy, what is set aside, what is "otherworldly." The desire of many people to see external signs of commitment—religious habits, medals and crosses—can come from a desire for clearer identity. People long to signify and express what is most important for them, their faith.

Yet we hear our churches referred to as "worship spaces," and we see in those spaces a lack of reverence that negates the sense of *sanctuary.* We see the Blessed Sacrament placed off to the side, often inconspicuously or ambiguously, so that people are no longer sure whether to bow or genuflect or just take a seat.

Churches once left open so that people could "make a visit" are now locked up like Fort Knox, and people are shooed out the door quickly after Mass so the priest can close up the church and get his breakfast. Perhaps we should lock our valuables somewhere else or put them in museums, so that our churches can once again become houses of prayer, houses of God (see Luke 19:46). During the Jubilee year, as I sought in vain for a church in which to pray before the Blessed Sacrament, I could not help but notice the irony expressed in the banner above a locked church door: "Open wide the doors to Christ!"

If *he is* really here—concretely, personally, the eternal Son come out to meet me, infinitely vulnerable to me in his passion and death, laid open for me to eat and drink—how can I be casual about Communion, as if I am at table anywhere with my friends? How can I not fall to my knees?

Enter In

Pope Benedict XVI touched upon the littleness with which we must enter into the mystery of the self-gift of Jesus in the Eucharist when he spoke to the college of cardinals the day after his election: "The Eucharist makes constantly present the Risen Christ who continues to give himself to us, calling us to participate in the banquet of his Body and his Blood. From full communion with him flows every other element of the Church's life: first of all, communion among all the faithful, the commitment to proclaiming and witnessing to the Gospel, the ardour of love for all, especially the poorest and lowliest."[1]

Yes, Jesus has truly become that intimate with us. He has given himself as our food and drink. The celebration of the Eucharist is our reception of Love himself, our receiving his flesh and blood into our flesh and blood.

At Mass do we really take the opportunity to talk to Christ? Is there any more intimate moment to do this than upon receiving him in the Eucharist? If we miss the intimacy of receiving him who has given himself completely to us, we fail to draw upon the power that lies right under our noses, right in our own tradition. The church gives us many avenues toward peace and intimacy, but we find it especially in the sacramental intimacy with the Lord that we have in the Eucharist.

Rather than spending our days rushing about, nervously talking to ourselves about what is going on or going wrong, let's take the opportunity to deepen our communion with the Lord whom we have received in Holy Communion. This ongoing communion with the Lord takes our prayer into a real relationship.

This may sound pious, but try it. We can have the fruit of union with Jesus and can commune with him personally, in words or in wordless love, rather than simply thinking about him or forgetting about him altogether. It might seem impossible because of all our obligations and preoccupations and our tendency to become absorbed in them. It might seem that it would require enormous willpower and self-discipline, which I know I lack. But for God all things are possible.

Is there someone you fell in love with? Do you remember how that person absorbed your thoughts to the point that you could think of nothing else? This is passion. And just like human love, love for the Lord involves more surrender and abandonment than it does control.

It does require giving up the search for a drug, a technique, the right self-help book, the latest quick fix, and instead spending time, seemingly wasting time, alone with the Lord. And more than being alone, I think it is being intimate with the Lord that scares us.

And since we have dared to receive his Body and Blood, now we must somehow enflesh him who has become incarnate and given himself to us. At the end of Mass we are sent forth to do precisely this. As Jesus said after washing the feet of his apostles, "If you know these things, blessed are you if you do them" (John 13:17).

The reception of the Eucharist should fundamentally change

how we see others and how we see ourselves. It should lead to a profound examination of how we live in charity with the neighbor we can see, as well as with those we cannot see but who are affected by our lifestyle, our use of resources, our generosity or lack thereof. We cannot receive the Body and Blood of Christ without entering into a deeper intimacy and responsibility for all the members of his body.

On the other hand, acts of charity are hollow unless they come from an interiority full of love, a love we cannot generate on our own but rather must receive in the most intimate gift of self made by the Son of God in the Eucharist. Then we have something to share that is more than our money, more than ourselves even. We can share in the self-gift of Christ in the Eucharist.

Prayer Before the Sacrament

To shrink and decrease in the process of conversion, it is absolutely necessary to spend time in quiet prayer daily, if possible for extended periods of time. It is undeniably true that the most powerful way to pray like this is before the Blessed Sacrament. Indeed, renewed devotion to the Eucharist has swept through our church in recent years, often initiated and supported by "little ones," including many converts. The love of basking in and being vulnerable in Christ's vulnerability has found expression in Eucharistic adoration.

Such devotion does not compete with but complements the celebration and reception of the Eucharist. Pope John Paul II stated, "The Eucharist is a priceless treasure: by not only celebrating it but also by praying before it outside of Mass we are enabled to make contact with the very wellspring of grace."[2]

I usually encourage skeptical people who demure in following this recommendation to dispense from justifying this devotion historically or theologically and just try it. Invariably they discover something intimately special about praying before the Blessed Sacrament. I suppose this mainly has to do with the real presence of our Lord. He is, of course, present everywhere, but he is *sacramentally* present here, in his body, blood, soul and divinity.

But since many are unable to resist asking questions about this type of prayer anyway, let's take a look at them. Why gaze upon the exposed Sacrament or upon a tabernacle, especially when I have already received him?

We have a human need to look, to see, to be near. There is undoubtedly a melting down, a vulnerability, that leaves many of us uncomfortable yet without which we cannot really grow more deeply in our relationship with Christ. It is always more tempting to read about him than to meet him, to think about him than to actually talk to him, and to talk to him all the time rather than to listen to him. We need in quiet to allow ourselves to realize the personal presence of him whom we have received. We should talk to him, connect with him, engage him in the most personal way possible.

This touches upon another objection some make to Eucharistic devotion: that it makes us too introspective, too individualistic in our relationship with God, thus less likely to face the real challenges of life and of relationships with others. But we need never fear that allowing ourselves to be alone with Jesus will lead to a self-centered spirituality of "me and Jesus," that we will forget our neighbor and the community, especially those who are most in need. The director of spiritual life at one seminary noted that the seminarians who voluntarily spent time in the chapel adoring the Sacrament each day were the same ones who signed up to help out at the food bank and at the homeless men's mission.

Prayer and any relationship require time. This is the meaning of the classical devotion of the "holy hour." Though Jesus reproached his apostles for not being able to stay awake and pray with him one hour (see Matthew 26:40–46), there is nothing magical about sixty minutes except that it suggests an extended time to allow things to happen, to allow the love of the one we have received to penetrate us. It is nearly impossible for some of us to sit still long enough to try this, which only demonstrates how urgent the need is to do it.

As anyone who has tried to pray in this way knows, if one perseveres and remains, the romantic glow fades. Faith is even tested as we wonder if this is all a hoax, if there is nothing here but bread, if we are wasting time in this church all by ourselves. Ideas about things we could be doing and other distractions can besiege us as we strive to concentrate in prayer.

Anyone who has been through the experience of living out a committed relationship, undertaking serious study or research, learning a language or how to play a musical instrument or a new game knows similar doubts and fears. Just as many in our times do not persevere long enough to see what happens if they remain in that troubled marriage, many do not enter deeply enough into prayer to outlast the dryness, the distractions, the doubts. Consequently they never get very deeply into a relationship with the Lord and never develop much interiority.

Perhaps that is why so many people in our times suffer from a sense that reality is not real. There is an overall feeling of meaninglessness because there is a sort of detachment from everything. Well, such feelings are accurate in that we do not have enough interiority to be attached or to give ourselves over in any depth to others or to God. Indeed, persevering in prayer, turning our attention again and again to the Lord and regaining a listening attentiveness to him, strengthens our attention for other relationships in which we are always being called upon to listen.

How should we persevere? The main thing we need to do is to simply stay there and prolong the prayer and devotion we had at the moment we received the Eucharist.

A Place for Vulnerability

Praying, before the Blessed Sacrament or anywhere else, requires vulnerability and passion, and these often blossom most when I am tired or "not in the mood." Trying too hard to focus is counterproductive. All I need to do is surrender and turn back to God again and again, making each return to him not an act of frustration but an act of love.

Even those who vie for places at the head table are trying to be close to the one who invited them, though they may not understand why. Yet the only way to really come close—whether to a human being or to the Lord—is to go to the lowest place, to become vulnerable.

I find it easier as time goes on to speak from my heart and to listen from the same place. I also find that the less seriously I take myself—the less I focus on myself and what I am getting out of this, the more I forget myself and focus on him—the better it goes. And I find it better to hold out before him whomever and whatever I am concerned about or distracted by rather than worrying about getting rid of distractions. What a welcome change of pace that is, and it is precisely the disposition I need to be poor and little before him!

When I forget myself, I am amazed at what he teaches me, and I am ready to hear and assimilate it because I have my head out of my navel! This is also the best way to prepare to offer him everything, even what I have to live on. It becomes easier to offer him everything as I adore him in the sacrament of his total self-gift in love!

Eucharistic devotion is not magical, because magic implies

control and manipulation, power over things. Nor is it a focus on externals, since it takes me to the threshold of the external and the internal and integrates them. The exposed Blessed Sacrament is not an object but a person who is infinitely self-emptying Love, giving himself, pouring himself out right before our eyes and right into us.

To adore our Lord in the Blessed Sacrament requires falling to my knees, realizing how small I am. Even more, it requires going out in faith and in smallness, offering myself to him who offers himself to me. The Incarnation is sometimes defined as a marvelous exchange whereby God shares in our humanity in order to give us a share in his divinity. The Eucharist allows us to embody this marvelous exchange.

As we assimilate what all this means, how could our disposition be any other than adoration? This is interpersonal communion of the most intimate kind, offered by God and received by us only in total powerlessness.

One day, toward the end of Pope John Paul II's life, one of his aides found him sitting in his altar chair in his private chapel. He had his arms around the tabernacle and was singing in Polish. The aide left the chapel but later asked the pope what he had been doing. Pope John Paul responded that he had been singing a song his mother used to sing to him as a boy when he was sad. He had been comforting our Lord.[3]

The marvelous exchange that the Lord initiates flows both ways if we are small enough to allow this intimacy and not be afraid of its passion. Let us take opportunities to contemplate this in the fullest sense, participating in the very life of him whom we have received. ❧

CHAPTER TEN

BEHOLD HIS FACE

They shall look on him whom they have pierced" (John 19:37).

Pope John Paul II over the years repeatedly encouraged us, especially young people, to seek the face of Christ.[1] As I mentioned previously, we can resist this call, going to great lengths to keep our relationship with Jesus indirect. This seems particularly to be true of the face of Jesus crucified. This is the very face of love itself, yet some people find the depiction of the sufferings of Christ to be abhorrent, almost obscene.

The cross is a source of scandal (see 1 Corinthians 1:17–29). Jews can see it as an instrument of the most despicable criminal execution but also as a sign of the persecution they have experienced at the hands of Christians. Many Christians have difficulty seeing a cross with a corpus, sometimes claiming that the Resurrection of Christ should supercede his passion and death. But theological reasons are usually mixed with other deep feelings.

Even Catholics, who are accustomed to seeing crucifixes in their churches, schools and homes, can recoil when they see a crucifix that realistically depicts the suffering, the wounds, the blood, the agony. There is a preference here for a symbolic depiction rather than a realistic one. Why is the realism repelling, even for those who believe and perhaps especially for them?

I connect to this the reaction people sometimes have to graphic depictions of an aborted fetus. We look away from these attempts to bring us face-to-face with the reality of murder in the womb. Similarly, we find it difficult to look at pictures of starving people. Yet blessed are the hungry, the persecuted, the poor in spirit, the meek, the least ones (see Matthew 5:3–12), hard as it is to gaze upon them. And when they are all embodied at one time in the person of Jesus Christ, especially if he is not depicted in his glory or in some other way that paints over the passion, then we have to look and see.

The obscenity of pornography lies in taking what ought to be intimate and exposing it, reducing a person to a mere object of lust. Is it the exposure, the naked truth, the violence done to what is beautiful and intimate, the abuse of love, that bothers us—or that ought to bother us— if we have not anesthetized ourselves to the obscenity through addiction?

In the name of freedom of expression, the world expects Christians to tolerate with open mind and good humor perversions of the symbols of their faith in a way that it expects no other group of believers to tolerate. The crucifix, though it is an object, represents the most intimate act of love possible. Thus distress is understandable if we see a crucifix bearing lacquered feces or a dead rat, as I once saw.

Perversion, even under the label of artistic expression, always wants to play with and abuse what otherwise would be too overwhelming for us to look upon and realize. There is something radically wrong with a man who passively allows his wife to be raped or even verbally violated, and there is something equally wrong with the indifference of a believer to sacrilege of sacraments and sacramentals.

The Suffering Christ

A woman told me that she had never seen such violence and hatred in a movie as she saw in *The Passion of the Christ.* (She must not see many movies!) But any violence and hatred in that movie was for me totally eclipsed by Christ's love. I marveled at how he seemed to want to take on more, to drink the cup to the dregs, to stand up and go further.

The depth of his suffering was apparent for me less in what was done by his tormentors and more by their eyes. They seemed to need each other for reinforcement, yet they never looked at anyone, especially Christ, directly in the eyes. When Christ's eyes met theirs, there was a fleeting disconcerting moment, then confusion, then looking away. Sin is like that.

The passion and the suffering of Christ go beyond any physical torture and occur most deeply in the wounds of vulnerable love being blindly scorned and abused. The movie sums up Jesus' response to this suffering when his mother catches up with him on his way to Calvary. As she looks into his agonized eyes, he simply says, almost with joy, "Look, Mother, I make all things new!" Here indeed is "the Lamb who was slain" (Revelation 5:12).

It is hard to understand how God, even the Son of God become human, can suffer. This is probably one of the obvious reasons why many people do not really believe that in Jesus Christ we have the eternal Son of God in person. They do not believe that he is eternally divine in every way that the Father is divine and has in time become human in every way that we are human.

How can God suffer? How can God die? Christ, while remaining always the eternal Son, emptied himself of his divinity or his divine prerogatives in some sense (see Philippians 2:7), but how did his divinity and humanity interplay in his passion? If he could see ahead to the Resurrection, how could he really suffer and die? How could he in any sense be vulnerable, capable of being wounded?

The church has never tried to exhaustively explain this mystery of love, simply because it cannot be exhaustively explained. So what we say here are only suggestions. The church has insisted that we cannot say that since he is God he did not really suffer and did not really die, that he only appeared to suffer and die and therefore only appeared to be human (docetism). Nor can we say that he stopped being God long enough to live and die and became God again, or that he became God for the first time (adoptionism) in his Resurrection.

It might help us to understand the passion of the divine Son if we remember what we have said earlier, that while God is omnipotent, omniscient, omnipresent and all the other "omnis," he is infinite, self-emptying Love. We can say that he is "omni-kenotic," "omni-vulnerable"! Here we are really talking about not only what Jesus suffered in his passion and death on the cross but the passion with which he entered into the Incarnation and with which he lived his whole life.

Was he affected as the Son of God by our sins, by the condition of those whom he met? Or was he somehow impassible? If the latter, he is without passion, not only in a human sense but also in any analogous divine sense. How can we then think of or imagine anything like divine concern or care? In fact, a God without passion, in some analogous sense to ours, a God who is unaffected or unconcerned, who doesn't care, would be a monster.

We cannot attribute to God human qualities that are sheer deficiencies, such as sinfulness, hatred, ignorance or illness. We *can*, however, attribute to him in an infinite, perfect way the good qualities that we have in a finite and even a deficient way. I would propose that rather than being impassible, incapable of feeling or of having passion as we human beings do, it would be more accurate to say that not only Christ but all three divine Persons are infinitely concerned, infinitely caring, infinitely affected by us— omni-passible, if you will.

God loves infinitely, pouring himself out infinitely and never being in the least exhausted by this, infinitely vulnerable and affected by everything without in the least being diminished by it all. This is how the three divine Persons love perfectly in their oneness. This is how God has loved and redeemed us through the Incarnation, passion and death of the Son.

The Infinite Passion

What did Jesus experience in his passion? Again, I offer not a definitive answer but only an attempt at understanding.

The infinite love that the Son expressed in his Person had to be poured out completely in a human way, all the way to death. Because he became one of us and because at the same time he is the eternal Son, he suffered the suffering of all, those who lived and died before him as well as those who lived during the span of his historical life and all those who will ever live. Likewise, he shared in human death and died a human death, and he has lived and suffered and died for and with everyone before and after him. Finally, though he is human like us in everything but sin (see Hebrews 4:15; Eucharistic Prayer IV), he took on the sin of all people of all time, and by his sacrifice he redeemed us all.

Try then to imagine the passion of an infinite being. At the height of his agony he could see not only the people who stood before him, jeering or weeping, but all the people of all time. He saw us in our loving and in our refusing to love, our sinning and our repenting. At the same eternal moment, he took on all the moments of every life and death. He could be the infinite love of God in person to each human being who ever lived and who ever will live.

He saw all of this, and he suffered in his humanity. He died not only in material poverty, his clothing auctioned by dice (see Matthew 27:35; John 19:24), but also in the poverty of total abandonment by those closest to him (Matthew 26:56). He experienced the refusal of divine love in the sin of all people of all time, not only in divine consciousness but also in human consciousness. Surely this suffering was greater than any physical suffering.

Those who did not flee from the cross, his mother and his beloved disciple (see John 19:25–27), he let go of and gave away too, entrusting them to each other. Mary, honored to be the human most intimate with God, gave him his human flesh, bore him in her womb, cradled him in her arms at birth and again at death. Jesus left her to be mother not only of his disciple but also of us all, indeed Mother of the Church. She gives us to Jesus as the brothers and sisters his passion has adopted, so that we can call his beloved Father our Father in this beloved Son.

I mentioned before the suffering I saw in the ocean of faces in a busy city in India. I am quite sensitive to the world's suffering and longing for God's love. Yet I am only sensitive in a limited way, and I could only see certain people at a certain distance. I could only imagine, probably very inaccurately, their experiences.

Imagine knowing it all, seeing it all, experiencing it all for all people of all time within infinite divine transparency and vulnerability! The silence that this mystery deserves recalls the silence in which Jesus died and breathed forth his Spirit.

The Suffering Son

I have not sufficiently expressed the deepest meaning of the mystery of Christ's passion and self-giving love. *How* he could suffer and die like this is one question. The more burning question is *why?* Out of love, of course, love for us and for our salvation.

Yet we must remember that what is revealed to us of God's love in Jesus Christ is an expression of the infinite love within God himself. He is in himself a communion of love, an interpersonal communion of such unlimited, perfect love that the three divine Persons are one. His mission to become incarnate, to empty himself and become a servant, one of us, is not his action alone and is not for us alone. It is a consequence of the way God loves, even within himself.

The Father sent the Son through the Holy Spirit, as revealed and confirmed at Jesus' baptism in the Jordan at the hand of Saint John the Baptist. The Spirit descended upon Jesus in the form of a dove, and from the heavens the voice of *Abba,* his beloved Father, proclaimed, "Thou art my beloved Son; with thee I am well pleased" (Luke 3:22). Here we see the intimacy between the Father and the Son, in the Holy Spirit, each Person in the Trinity active in a way personal to him.

We have said that of all the titles given to Jesus, he himself seemed to emphasize in his own preaching the suffering Son of Man, who is servant. The heart of this title is the word *Son.* The most compelling feature of his life and ministry is the intimacy Jesus has as beloved Son of the Father.

So what about Jesus' relationship with his Father as he suffered and died on the cross? Already I have stretched in trying to imagine the suffering, passion and love of Jesus Christ. Did he suffer most by having a veil of infinite darkness pass between him and his Father? Are we to take literally his words from the cross "My God, my God, why hast thou forsaken me?" (Matthew 27:46)?

Or rather did he silently continue praying Psalm 22, a song of praise for the unfailing love of the Father? I believe he knew and experienced this infinite love in unveiled divine vulnerability, in infinite transparency, while he suffered humanly all the sin and failure to love of all people of all time.

This intimacy between the Father and the Son surely remained unbroken through the agony and abandonment. There the Son suffered precisely in knowing and being the infinite divine love poured out totally, in absolute transparency to our limited love or our sinful and rejecting failure to love. He poured himself out not only for us but also in obedient love of his Father, as the beloved Father poured himself out in sending his only begotten Son.

Throughout Jesus' life, surely in the full expression of his passion, he remained in total, infinite, loving relationship with his Father. This is the relationship manifested throughout his life in his prayer and communion with the Father. Indeed, Jesus died praying, "Father, into thy hands I commit my spirit" (Luke 23:46). The three divine Persons are revealed no more fully than at this moment, when they pour out their infinite love.

The Descent Into Hell

Jesus did not immediately return to the right hand of his Father after his death, and the Holy Spirit he breathed forth did not yet descend upon the church. First Jesus descended among the dead, into hell.

This descent is one of the most fascinating teachings of the faith in terms of its significance for his passion. It is documented rather emphatically in the First Letter of Saint Peter (4:6). Throughout the ages it has been understood in various ways. Some have seen it as the opening of the gates of heaven and the announcement of the Good News to those who had not had the chance to hear it, since they lived and died before Christ. Others have seen in it the penetration of the passion of Jesus Christ and his redemption even to the depths of hell, so that the damned too might know of Christ's victory. Surely it indicates that Christ conquers even the most unspeakable evil, even the most total desolation and godlessness.

Dare we hope then that somehow this victory will allow all people to be saved? Will even the damned get a last chance?

Many theologians have explored this idea, and Hans Urs von Balthasar, in *Dare We Hope "That All Men Will Be Saved"?*[2] traces the history of this conviction throughout the centuries. He says that we must hope in our own time that all will be saved, somehow in the dispensation of God's mercy and justice. Pope John Paul II echoes this conviction in *Crossing the Threshold of Hope*, while insisting that humans are free to refuse forgiveness and salvation.[3]

In the last chapter I will examine some of the questions of eternal life, purgatory and resurrection. Here I simply note the oft-forgotten final phase of the passion of Jesus Christ. Upon consummating his mission on earth through his suffering, he commended himself totally to his Father, breathing forth the Holy Spirit (John 19:30), shedding the last blood and water from his side and descending into hell. These events surely indicate the beginning of the church.

They also signify the importance of the time between the death of Jesus and his Resurrection. This was not simply a time of waiting and of faith being tested; it was time for the seed that had fallen into the ground and died to begin to germinate.

The effects of each moment of the life and death of Jesus Christ flow into every moment of time. This is particularly true of the days and hours of his passion, death and burial. All those who have ever lived are affected by what he has done, by his infinite vulnerability or passibility.

The moments of the Last Supper and the passion and death of Jesus Christ, as well as his descent into hell and his Resurrection, flow into the moments of each celebration of the Eucharist. We are not merely remembering, nor surely are we repeating, what was done at the Last Supper and on Calvary. Rather we are participating in those acts and their saving power by *anamnesis*, recalling them to mind. As he promised then, he is *with us* in our celebrations, and the redemption and eternal life that are his gift are ours now in our own time, all the more so as the Spirit allows us to truly "see and hear" (Acts 2:33). ❧

CHAPTER ELEVEN

THE VICTORY OF THE LAMB

$\mathbf{S}$ee my hands and my feet, that it is I myself; handle me, and see; for a spirit has not flesh and bones as you see that I have" (Luke 24:39; see John 20:27).

We have already commented on the essential connection between our faith in the bodily Resurrection of Jesus and our faith in his Incarnation and in his real presence in the Eucharist. Certainly the faith of the church insists upon all three of these.

Jesus Christ has risen from the dead and has promised that we will rise with him! Let us first try to understand the meaning of his Resurrection and then consider our participation in it.

Flesh and Bones

We are not to understand Jesus' bodily Resurrection as a mere resuscitation of a corpse. The raising of Lazarus (see John 11) and of the son of the widow of Nain (see Luke 7:11–15) were resuscitations of people who presumably died again later on. Likewise those who rose from the dead in the earthquake at the death of Jesus returned to the grave to await the general resurrection at the end of time (see Matthew 27:52–53).

Jesus, however, was so transformed in his Resurrection that he was often not immediately recognizable. The accounts of his appearances are strikingly sober. Faith was needed to bridge the gap between his glorified appearance and his earthly body, though the glorified body still had an ordinary quality to it. As Saint Paul says, the earthly body is sown in death, and the spiritual body rises in the resurrection (see 1 Corinthians 15:35–50).

Just as the grain of wheat falls into the ground and dies and then transforms into what germinates and sprouts (see John 12:24), so everything we have been and are in our lives will be transformed and raised in the resurrection from the dead. Jesus insisted upon this when he appeared to his disciples after his Resurrection. Though he seemed to appear out of nowhere and then disappear, perhaps in another experience of divine transparency, he insisted that he was not a ghost. He had them touch him, and he asked them for food, which they could watch him eat so they might see his bodiliness.

The accounts of the risen Lord's appearances may have been written to refute the tendency of gnosticism to deny the bodily Resurrection of Jesus, but they surely reflect historical reality. Though there seem to have been some rumors that the apostles stole the body, no one seems to have questioned whether the tomb was really empty. Saint Paul says that "if Christ has not been raised, then our preaching is in vain and your faith is in vain" (1 Corinthians 15:14).

If the bones of Jesus were discovered tomorrow, or if they were eaten by dogs from a mass grave, as one historical critic supposes, this would destroy the meaning of the Incarnation and its fruit, which is harvested in the Resurrection. Like the gnostic tendency of some early Christians to devalue all that is material and bodily, even to consider it sinful or evil, so the gnostics of today consider the physicality of our bodiliness nonessential and irrecoverable in the resurrection.

The decomposition of the bodies of the dead, if they are not cremated first, does seem to present a problem. How do all those molecules that have, according to the principle of conservation of matter moved on to become parts of other bodies, regroup for the resurrection of the physical body of a particular individual?

This type of thinking actually shows how little we understand about the body and matter, much less about spirit or mind or soul. And if, as contemporary physics tells us, matter is not stuff but energy, it is easy to consider that there may be many transformations that conserve matter in ways that the natural sciences have not figured out. This is all the more likely given the fact that resurrection is a supernatural process!

Our eventual bodily resurrection makes sense if our bodiliness is essentially human, as we have seen Pope John Paul II insist in his theology of the body. Everything we are and have been will be picked up and preserved, including our bodiliness. Our mode of being in eternal life will probably have more to do with the way we have given ourselves in love and have been received rather than our present physical makeup.

This self-giving is what Pope John Paul calls our "nuptial capacity," which he considers to be essentially bodily and sexual.[1] In eternal life we will not give and receive each other in marriage as do husbands and wives on earth (see Luke 20:34–36), but our eternal existence will have much to do with how we have come to live in Christ and how we have come to live in each other in him. The Resurrection of Jesus Christ is the first revelation of what this will be like.

The Risen Lord's Wounds

Among the other significant details of the appearances of our risen Lord is the fact that, despite the glorification of his body, there is none of the splendor found in his transfiguration before Peter, James and John on the mountain (see Luke 9:28–36). He appears so ordinary that he can be mistaken for a gardener (John 20:15). Moreover, in at least some accounts of his appearances, he presents the emblems of his passion, his wounds, as credentials. This seeming detail emphasizes the fact that his disciples recognize him not by superficial resemblance but by getting to the heart of the meaning of who he is. He has suffered, died and risen. He is the Lord of the passion!

Passion always seeks to be explicit, to be concrete, as we have observed. Jesus went ahead of his disciples to Jerusalem, and he came to meet them (see Luke 24:13–35). He gave them peace and the Holy Spirit, then extended the forgiveness of sins and the power to forgive sins (John 20:21–23). This is the same forgiveness that opened up and healed the deepest needs of all those who came to him for healing during his earthly ministry. Only the one who has forgiven everyone everything by taking it upon himself can delegate others to offer that forgiveness.

Again we encounter the doubt that fears this is too good to be true. Passion wants to see with its own eyes. Saint Thomas is the one who has the passion to doubt and the passion to demand to see and to touch (see John 20:24–29).

Ultimately, faith has to believe beyond what can be seen and touched, but Jesus became one of us so we could touch him, see him, eat him and drink him. We can respond to his offering only if we are vulnerable enough to touch him in his most vulnerable spots, to look upon him whom we have pierced, to penetrate those wounds by putting our fingers into the nail marks and our hand into his side. We need to be vulnerable enough to place our wounds against his, to let his blood flow from his body into our most vulnerable parts, into our own body and blood.

Saint Thomas cried out, "My Lord and my God!" (John 20:28). Recently I was proclaiming this gospel at a funeral of a nun who had taught me in grade school, and I found that the word *Lord* had been whited-out and replaced with the word *savior.* When I asked about this later, I was told that the liturgist had taken this step because the word *Lord* evokes a sense of patriarchal hierarchy and dominance.

I was and am still surprised. Saint Thomas proclaimed Jesus his Lord and his God in praise of the wounds, in praise of the vulnerability of his self-giving love! Any power exercised in the name of Jesus must be humble like this. The lordship of Jesus Christ corrects all the abusive forms of lordship, even if his all too human followers often forget this.

We see this acknowledgment also in the ancient hymn Saint Paul cited in his Letter to the Philippians (see Philippians 2:6–11). We proclaim that Jesus Christ is Lord by bending the knee in a way that echoes the acknowledgment of the lordship of Yahweh in Isaiah 45:23. Jesus is worthy of worship as Yahweh is. He did not cling to his equality with God but was vulnerable enough to empty himself and become a servant, one of us.

This is how Jesus changed the meaning of lordship in all the expectations of those awaiting the Messiah, the anointed one, the Christ. He is Lord because of his self-emptying obedience, his lowliness, his willingness to serve, to give himself. This is what the risen Lord most of all wanted to proclaim in the glory and transformation of his Resurrection. His promise that we will share in his Resurrection is an invitation to share in his self-giving love.

The Glory That Is to Come

We now live between Christ's death and Resurrection and our own death and Resurrection. In baptism we died with him so that we might rise with him (see 2 Timothy 2:11). We are deepened in this mystery each time we receive the sacraments and allow these mysteries to take flesh in us—in our lives, in our loves and certainly in our prayer. The Eucharist especially is our way of celebrating and participating in what Christ has already done. His life flows into these moments of our lives, and we live in joyful hope of his coming again in glory to complete and fulfill all that he has done.

This is the church on earth, and the church as a people still on pilgrimage. Jesus has ascended in glory, in his incarnate and glorified risen being, to the right hand of the Father. Yet he remains present with us all our days, most powerfully in the Eucharist. The Holy Spirit dwells in us in a special way now that we have become the body of Christ, and it is the Holy Spirit who brings us into the intimacy between the Father and the Son.

Jesus promises that he will come again in glory, that our death will not be alone but can be in him and that we will share his Resurrection. Two thousand years after the death and Resurrection of Jesus, we still pray, *Maranatha.* Come, Lord Jesus!

Scott Hahn, in his brilliant book *The Lamb's Supper,* traces through the tradition of the church the deepest meaning of the Book of Revelation: that the *parousia* is now, that Jesus is here in his fullness as heaven and earth come together in the Mass. The celebration of the Eucharist uncovers the victory of the Lamb who was slain. The word *apocalypse* means "an unveiling," a revealing for the judgment and the mercy of all.[2]

There has been speculation from earliest times about when the end will come and what Jesus will look like when he comes, about where we will be when the trumpet sounds and how we will all be assembled and judged. The battles, monsters and signs in the Book of Revelation surely can disclose much that was to come in the times in which John wrote as well as in our own times. But the deeper meaning lies in the *apocalypse,* the uncovering, the unveiling of the Lamb who has been slain. "They shall look on him whom they have pierced" (John 19:37)!

Now, inescapably, we must gaze, we must touch, we must expose ourselves in total vulnerability to the love the Father has shown to us through Jesus Christ and the victory he has won. A

Lamb has saved us. How fitting! One of the least of the animals, even the poor shepherds in Bethlehem had them. The Good Shepherd has saved all his lost sheep by becoming one of them!

The One offering the sacrifice has himself become the sacrifice. The Lamb who has been slain is the Shepherd who leads all the sheep to God, who wipes every tear from their eyes (see Revelation 7:17). The Good Shepherd lays down his life for his sheep, not merely by carrying the lost lamb on his shoulders and defending the sheep but by becoming himself a sheep, a living sacrifice, both priest and victim. This is how he is revealed in the Book of Revelation, bringing to a definitive end all the battles, the power of Satan, the martyrdom of the just.

I think of the parable of the servants to whom the master entrusted talents. The servant who buried his talents did so out of fear, believing his master to be a harsh and unjust man who wanted to reap where he did not sow (see Luke 19:22–23). Many people think of God that way, despite what has been revealed in Jesus Christ. Contrast this story with that of the woman who persevered in demanding justice though she knew the judge to be unjust. This woman received what she was seeking (see Luke 18:1–8)!

Perhaps as we come to share in the divine patience, hopefully during life but if not, then in purgatory, our distortions and sinful ways of seeing God will be transformed. After all the battles, after all the temptations of Satan and the debauchery of sin, after all the fears of divine wrath and justice, we will see him as the Lamb who was slain out of love for us, the Good Shepherd who loves each of his sheep as if each is the only one, the Shepherd who turns out after all to be a Lamb.

Jesus uncovers himself before us all at the end. He shows us who he really is, how he really loves and thereby who we are to him. He comes not to inflict suffering but to appeal to us to seek healing for our wounds in his wounds, to confess and be forgiven. The feared divine wrath is unveiled as the passionate self-giving love of the beloved Father. Saint Paul wrote to the Corinthians, "Now the Lord is the Spirit, and where the Spirit of the Lord is, there is freedom. And we all, with unveiled face, beholding the glory of the Lord, are being changed into his likeness from one degree of glory to another; for this comes from the Lord who is the Spirit" (2 Corinthians 3:17–18). Patience and vulnerability in his patience and vulnerability make us transparent in his transparency. 🙠

CHAPTER TWELVE

THE LAST THINGS

The Catholic church has the tradition that each person will experience a particular judgment at the moment of death and will participate in the general judgment at the end of time. We do not have a lot of clear revelation about these things, especially in sacred Scripture, so again what we say here is largely speculative.

Since every moment of time is flooded by the moments of the passion, death and Resurrection of Jesus Christ, we can really believe that it is possible through baptism to live in him, to suffer in his suffering and ultimately to die in his death so that we will one day rise in his rising. Indeed, in his passion Jesus Christ actually suffered our suffering and took on our sin. He experienced this and bore this for each individual who would ever live. And in his dying he died the death of each one of us. Then, in descending among the dead, we can imagine that he meets each one of us individually in our death, in the moment of his own suffering and death on the cross, face-to-face with us, unveiled!

Particular Judgment and Purgatory

Taylor Caldwell wrote a novel some years ago called *He Who Listens.* A man leaves provision in his will for a place to be built and available to anyone at any time who needs someone to listen. Various persons in time of need go there to meet the one who listens. Each one sits in the waiting room for a certain length of time, then enters another room where there is only a chair facing a curtain, behind which apparently is sitting the one who listens.

The person, after going through some awkwardness or uncertainty, begins to talk, eventually pouring out rage, hurt, bitterness, fear, sorrow, regret, repentance, hope. Sometimes he or she pleads and argues for a response from the one who listens. Finally the curtain is drawn back, and the person falls into deep peace before the crucifix.

The crucifixion, the passion and death of our Lord Jesus Christ, unveils, exposes and frees. In the particular judgment Christ will unveil his identification not only with humanity as a whole but also with me, his lost sheep. I will see myself in light of his passion, at the intersection of the moment of his death with the moment of my death. I will see myself as I truly am. I will not be able to look away but will have to look at the unveiled love of him whom I have pierced, for he will still bear those wounds as the emblems of his love.

Purgatory offers us the opportunity for purgation, for purification, after our first death. There is nothing to fear in this except fear itself, if it keeps us from contrition and from accepting Christ's love.

We know that those in purgatory are part of the body of Christ. They cannot help themselves but benefit from our prayers and sacrificial love. This makes sense when we consider that the purification most people need is from all the false senses of self-sufficiency, self-righteousness and self-centeredness that keep us from being truly self-giving. Refusal to be children of God is what leads to sin. In purgatory souls can learn how to be little children, how to be poor, how to recognize themselves as the least and the lowest. They can learn to receive love as grace, for free, to accept what others give and how they love.

I personally believe that few of us are abandoned in childlike trust so totally as to be ready to enter into the fullness of the transparent glory of God's infinitely self-giving love when we die. We don't have the capacity to receive that love, so purgatory gives us the opportunity to expand our hearts, to become self-emptying, to become transparent.

Perhaps some of the ghosts that people report seeing are actually the souls of purgatory haunting the world in which they lived, stuck and unresolved in some very fundamental ways. Movies like *Ghost, Flatliners* and *Sixth Sense* are highly intuitive of these realities, though the need for purgation can be understood fully only when the dead see themselves in relationship with the Crucified One, the Lamb who was slain.

There seem to be persons who have a particular vocation to pray for and help, and indeed even to see and get to know personally, the suffering ones in purgatory. But the only way to be a "ghost buster" is to come to understand and live self-giving love with passion and vulnerability, in Jesus Christ. Then we can stay prayerfully aware of the members of the mystical body of Christ in purgatory.

We are purified through Christ's passion and self-giving love either now or later, either in this life or in purgatory. What a wonderful gift this is. My dear friend Father Benedict Groeschel often used to end his letters with "I will see you soon—and if not, then I will see you in purgatory." Yet Father Groeschel insists that we should pray not to go to purgatory but to go to heaven, to die to self now so that our hearts are expanded to become ready to enter one day into the fullness of the infinite love of God.

The fear that haunts us throughout our lives arises from the sense that we really are not living as we should, that we are avoiding what is most important, that we are missing the point altogether. We have a sense that we are living behind a veil, and we do not know how to remove it. Actually, it has already been removed.

We need only be willing to be reborn, to become again like little children, to remember who we are so that we can realize whom we have become in his passion.

Jesus stands at the door and knocks. There seems to be opportunity for purgation beyond the particular judgment. Let us hope that at the moment of his full revelation we will all cry out with the martyrs and saints, proclaiming the glory of the Lamb who was slain.

The General Judgment

The tragic occurrences in the Book of Revelation are like bad dreams from which we awake when the Lamb who has been slain appears. Not only is he revealed and uncovered as who he really is, but we too are unveiled as who we really are. This is the judgment.

For those who persist in their sin, the Lamb will seem a harsh and unjust master who reaps where he did not sow. Yet how could one fail, seeing his wounds and his vulnerability, to realize how much he has sown and how good the seed is? That good seed is the gift of faith, and he comes only to reap what he has sown!

As in the parable of the sower and the seed (see Luke 8:5–15), the seed is good, but the land upon which it is sown is sometime unable to receive it. Perhaps the soil is too hard, too full of weeds or thorns, leaving the seed lying open to be trampled upon. But our sower does not merely sow the seed and leave it lying there vulnerable. He becomes vulnerable. The passion of Jesus Christ is exactly how the soil is plowed and made fertile, how the hard places are cleared or broken open. If we share that passion, the good seed sown in us can fall into the ground and die, to be rooted deeply rather than superficially, to flourish and grow, to be protected against the weeds and power of Satan.

But "when the Son of man comes, will he find faith on

earth?" (Luke 18:8). We must become like little children if we are to be seated with the other children at the wedding feast of the Lamb. This is the price of admission, the wedding garment we have to put on. Jesus himself has shown us the way.

It is amazing that in *his* victory he throws a feast for *us!* Like the prodigal father who lavished not only his wealth but also his mercy upon his prodigal son, he has readied for us a banquet (see Luke 15:11–32). The self-righteous ones, like the older son in the parable of the prodigal, miss the feast because they are waiting for a different kind of invitation, a different way in. They are waiting for an invitation that recognizes their service rather than one that comes as sheer gift from the gracious and passionate Lord of mercy and vulnerability. "Son, you are always with me, and all that is mine is yours" (Luke 15:31).

Jesus pleads passionately in his parables and other teachings that we stay awake, that we not miss the banquet. If I am occupied with my own concerns, I will be too busy to accept the invitation. I will be too far from the lowest and least to realize what I am refusing when I insist upon my own terms. Thus those in the highways and byways, the lame and the destitute, the helpless and the hopeless, even prostitutes and sinners, may be in a better position to hear and respond to the invitation to the banquet of the Lamb because they know they have nothing.

I am reminded again of the celebration of the Eucharist in Brazil with hundreds of brothers and sisters of the poor and the many poor and homeless they brought with them. It was chaotic, but there was no question that it was all about the Lamb who was slain, who was sharing himself with us in the Eucharist and who was all our joy and reason for being there. It is he who called us all together from all over the place, from the streets and even from the other side of the equator, to celebrate the wedding feast of the Lamb. Everyone was welcome; all he has is ours.

If I refuse the invitation, perhaps it is because I am looking for a feast celebrating myself or celebrating him in a different way. Maybe I never believed that he could be coming to wed *me*. What if I am unable to accept this personal intimacy with God? What if I am unable to believe that God is not merely absolute perfection in control of everything but also infinite, self-giving love? What if it seems too good to be true or does not fit my reasoning, my theology or my agenda?

What if I look condescendingly at the call to become the least out of love? What if I cannot believe that true wisdom is the wisdom of a little child, that I have to be reborn instead of working so hard to perpetuate the illusion that I am in control and know what I'm doing? What if I cannot believe that he would love me in total identification with me, even giving himself to the point of death? What if I have worked so hard to protect myself from being wounded that I do not want to gaze upon his wounds?

Then how shall I recognize him when he comes? How shall I recognize him now in others, especially in the least, and in myself who am truly least? How shall I ever live, how shall I ever love, how shall I ever die if not in him?

In the end he will be revealed in all his vulnerability, in all his littleness and in all his love. It will be impossible not to recognize him, but it will be possible still to reject him.

The Kingdom of Heaven

Once I had an allergic reaction leading to anaphylactic shock, and I became overwhelmed with the feeling that I was dying. I was surprised that I was not the least bit afraid to let go of everything and everyone, and indeed I felt as if everything and everyone were slipping away. As they say, my whole life passed before my eyes.

I realized that all that would last would be the love I have given and received, the ways I have given myself and been received by other persons. Nothing of value would be lost. The only shadow of regret I experienced was that often I had not loved well; I had been too afraid or selfish. But even this I knew would be forgiven.

At the same time I sensed that I was supposed to live longer, that there was more for me to do and give and learn. So I simply did not let myself fall into the love and surrender, and shortly I regained my ability to breathe and to focus.

If we want to imagine what heaven is like, I think we have to do it in the light of passion: seeing each other in transparency of love. We will be transparent as we share in the divine, infinite vulnerability and mercy of God in the most deeply personal way. Those persons whom we actually have known and loved, to whom we have given ourselves, will somehow be eternally in us and we in them in a most intimately personal way. Even those we have never known but whom we have touched or prayed for, or who have touched or prayed for us, will somehow be in us too and we in them, all in Christ and in God. If we are vulnerable and childlike, even now we can experience such transparency, as Mother Teresa said, "one Jesus at a time."

There is a joy and goodness that can only be known and lived by those who are very small, who know they are the least and do not mind it because they don't measure that way. "Blessed are the meek, for they shall inherit the earth" (Matthew 5:5). And woe to anyone who leads such a little one astray (see Luke 17:1–2), who robs a child of his or her innocence!

Little ones like this are everywhere but usually are found together, most comfortable on the margins of things without quite knowing that is where they are. They are mostly unafraid to ask for exactly what they need, and they have an intuition that leads them directly to those who can help them, guide them and love them. These are the ones who will be first in the kingdom, even if they have many weaknesses and have sinned much, because their whole lives have been a repentance and have brought others to repentance. They are the transparent ones, the ones who have given everything.

The director of the Vatican press office, Joaquin Navarro-Valls, reported that as Pope John Paul II lay dying, he said: "I have looked for you. Now you have come to me. And I thank you."[1] Interpretations of these words include the impression that the pope was thinking he was once again celebrating a Mass at a World Youth Day or speaking to thousands of young people gathered in St. Peter's Square. I opine that, in his transparency and his vulnerability, in his love for the little ones, he could already see coming to meet him those who have become like little children, the citizens of the kingdom of the beloved Father.

Come to the Banquet!

The pure of heart are blessed, for they will see God (see Matthew 5:8). Through the Son we are taken in the Holy Spirit into the glory of the Father, into the eternal life of the Trinity (see Ephesians 1:1–3). The Father will be revealed in all his glory as the beloved Father, through the wounds and vulnerability, through the passion and Resurrection of his Son.

The Holy Spirit is the transparency that allows all this to be uncovered, to be unveiled. In pouring himself out, the Spirit unveils that the Father and the Son are one. As we see the Lamb who was slain, the beloved Son, we will see the Father.

And to the degree that our passion has been lived in the passion of Jesus Christ, in a life of loving and self-emptying in his loving and self-emptying, we will be one with the Son eternally and will behold eternally the glory of the Father in his infinite outpouring of himself. Indeed, the only possible way to be in each other eternally lies in being in the Son, seeing him and loving him, then seeing and loving in his love. There is no love but love in him.

There is no eternal life but in his life, as we have already begun to taste by living in his grace on earth. What we see now veiled under the appearances of bread and wine we will see unveiled, in one eternal act of transparent, vulnerable love. Our life then will be in the Trinity, an intimate sharing in the infinitely self-giving love among the divine Persons, loving one another only in this transparency and in this self-gift.

Who would have thought that the end of it all would be a wedding feast of love, with me as the one being married? Who would have thought that the Bridegroom would become the feast, that judgment would end in nuptials? Who would have thought that our nuptial capacity would end in the wedding feast of the Lamb?

Even now the banquet has begun, even as the church in the midst of the sufferings of the world continues to cry out, "Come, Lord Jesus" (Revelation 22:20). We celebrate it in communion with all the angels and saints, with those in purgatory as well as all those on earth, in the celebration of the Eucharist. There the banquet in heaven is one with the banquet on earth.

Not all are seated yet at the table. We participate in the Lamb's sacrifice when we wash the feet of others and help them find a place at the banquet table. We need to abandon all worry about saving our seats in order to help them, even giving them our own seat. The example comes from the Lamb who was slain. He is not seated in the place of honor at the head of the table because he is *on* the table, *on* the altar, as the one who offers himself in love.

How privileged we are to be already partaking of this wedding feast, even before we are fully prepared! We need this food and drink, his flesh and blood. In it we can become more profoundly one in him, the Lamb who was slain. ❧

NOTES

Chapter One: In Search of Passion

1. Pope John Paul II, homily of May 11, 1991.

2. Pope Benedict XVI, Inaugural Mass Homily, April 24, 2005.

3. Victor Hugo, *The Hunchback of Notre Dame* (New York: Random, 1996), p. 298.

4. Summa I–II, Q. 24a 1, 4; Saint Thomas discusses the passions in I–II, Q. 22–48.

5. Saint Augustine, *Confessions,* Book I, Paragraph 1.

Chapter Two: The Passion of the New Evangelization

1. John Paul II, Apostolic Letter *Novo Millennio Ineunte* ("At the Beginning of the Third Millenium"), January 6, 2001, 40.

Chapter Three: Born Again

1. Saint Louis de Montfort, *True Devotion to Mary* (Bayshore, N.Y.: Montfort, 1957), p. 12.

Chapter Four: Childlike Loving and Living

1. Pope Benedict XVI, Inaugural Mass Homily, April 24, 2005.

Chapter Five: Faith the Size of a Mustard Seed

1. C.S. Lewis, *A Grief Observed* (New York: Bantam, 1988), p. 89.

2. John Paul II, *The Theology of the Body: Human Love in the Divine Plan* (Boston: Pauline, 1997), p. 35.

Chapter Six: Faith and Passionate Giving

1. Pope Benedict XVI, Inaugural Mass Homily.

Chapter Seven: The Passion of the Trinity

1. John Paul II, *The Theology of the Body,* pp. 25–102.

Chapter Eight: Jesus Christ: The Divine Becomes Human

1. Jacques Dupuis and Josef Neuner, eds., *The Christian Faith in the Doctrinal Documents of the Catholic Church* (Statan Island, N.Y.: Alba, 1983), p. 201.

2. Dupuis and Neuner, p. 6.

3. Dupuis and Neuner, p. 154.

4. Dupuis and Neuner, pp. 157, 160.

5. Dupuis and Neuner, p. 146.

6. Dupuis and Neuner, pp. 158–163.

7. Dupuis and Neuner, pp. 172–173.

8. For an excellent critique of some of these reductionistic approaches to the Gospels, see Luke Timothy Johnson, *The Real Jesus: The Misguided Quest for the Historical Jesus and the Truth of the Traditional Gospels* (San Francisco: Harper, 1997).

9. Pontifical Biblical Commission, *Scripture and Christology* (1984).

10. Pontifical Biblical Commission, *The Uses of Scripture in the Church*, 1993.

Chapter Nine: Real Food, Real Drink, Real Presence

1. First Message of His Holiness Benedict XVI at the end of the Eucharistic Concelebration with the Members of the College of Cardinals in the Sistine Chapel, April 20, 2005, 4.

2. John Paul II, Encyclical Letter *Ecclesia de Eucharistia* ("On the Eucharist in Its Relationship to the Church"), April 17, 2003, 25.

3. Robert Reilly, "Fearless: How John Paul II Changed the Political World," *Crisis,* May 2005, p. 27.

Chapter Ten: Behold His Face

1. John Paul II, Apostolic Letter *Novo Millennio Ineunte* ("At the Beginning of the Third Millennium"), January 6, 2001.

2. Hans Urs von Balthasar, *Dare We Hope "That All Men Be Saved"? With a Short Discourse on Hell* (San Francisco: Ignatius, 1988).

3. John Paul II, *Crossing the Threshold of Hope* (New York: Knopf, 1994), pp. 194–195.

Chapter Eleven: The Victory of the Lamb

1. John Paul II, *The Theology of the Body,* pp. 60–63.

2. Scott Hahn, *The Lamb's Supper* (New York: Doubleday, 1999), p. 122.

Chapter Twelve: The Last Things

1.   Joaquin Navarro-Valls, Holy See Press Officer, press release of April 2, 2005.